PHANTOM STRESS

PHANTOM STRESS

Brain Training To Master Relationship Stress

PHILLIP ROMERO, MD
with Joe LaPlaca

All persons in the case histories presented in this book are fictional composites inspired by actual cases used to illustrate the theories and methods of the author.

This book was printed in the United States of America.

To order additional copies of this book, contact:
Xlibris Corporation
1-888-795-4274
www.Xlibris.com
Orders@Xlibris.com
76056

CONTENTS

To my father, Mario
and my daughter, Sayume

Acknowledgments

My daughter, Sayume, sustained me with her love, patience, and support throughout this project. My coauthor, Joe LaPlaca, has steadfastly guided, prodded, challenged, and validated this project from its beginnings.

Particular thanks to all the professionals, neuroscientists, and colleagues whose work has inspired me over the past two decades. Special thanks to Bruce McEwen and Alfred E. Mirsky, professor of neuroendocrinology at Rockefeller University and member of the Board of Governors at the New York Academy of Sciences, who validated this project very early on and generously responded to my requests for scientific guidance. Encouragement from Mike Posner, Joseph LeDoux, Robert Sapolsky, Michael Meaney, Isabel Peretz, and Torres Theorell was invaluable. The work of Antonio Damasio, Richard Davidson, Paul Ekman, Eric Kandel, Sir Michael Rutter, Jeffrey Schwartz, Daniel Schacter, and Daniel Goleman guided me. The many scientists who presented their works at conferences of the New York Academy of Sciences inspired me.

Further thanks to Jigme Tsarong, the former director of the Tibetan Medical Center in India, and the writings of the Dalai Lama.

One of my biggest sources of inspiration has come from the many patients who worked with me and helped me realize that these tools could be effective in rapidly identifying and navigating stress. I can now take the battle with phantom stress to the public.

Special thanks to Fiamma Montagu for her editing skills and Rebecca Fox for her copy editing.

Preface

*P*hantom *Stress* presents Logosoma Brain Training, a method I developed to help my patients—individuals, couples, and families—battle the ravages of chronic stress in their relationship with themselves, with each other, and with the world. I created Logosoma Brain Training in the mid-1980s from my life's study and work. For more than thirty years, I have devoted myself to the study of human relationships in health and illness, the neurobiology of attachment and stress, and creative resilience to life's problems.

I began writing this book in 1997 during my recovery from illness and divorce, the consequences of my own chronic stress. In 2005, I was diagnosed with a metastatic Stage IV cancer and was confronted with my own mortality as never before. During my cancer treatment and recovery, my understanding of stress, the meaning of my life, and the importance of love and connectedness for resilience to stress were amplified. This book is about the stresses that can disconnect us from the meaning of our lives and threaten our most precious asset, connection with our own body and with those we love. I believe that through Logosoma Brain Training, we can tap into the miraculous, resilient nature of our bodies and that we can reconnect with each other the attachments that give our lives meaning.

Introduction

PHANTOM STRESS—REWIRING YOUR BRAIN FOR RESILIENCE TO STRESS

The column of crawling traffic seems endless. It has hardly moved in the last forty-five minutes. You're definitely going to be late. The sun is beating down on the roof of your car. "Why didn't I fix the air-conditioning last week?" Horns blare, and tempers flare. The heat and frustration combine to trigger a cascade of stress hormones in your body. Despite your efforts to remain calm, your mind is suddenly hijacked by a stream of negative thoughts. "I'm sure the boss didn't get my message about the traffic. He's always had it in for me. Now I'm definitely going to be fired! How will I pay the mortgage payments then? I'll be forced to go bankrupt. I'll lose everything. My partner will leave me. My family and friends will disown me! I'll end up totally alone! My life will be over!" Your cell phone rings, snapping you back to reality. You refocus on the moment. There's a message. It is your boss. The meeting's off! He sends his apologies: "Take the day off and go to the beach . . . you deserve it!" You wonder how you could have been so wrong. And why did a little traffic get you so upset?

PHANTOM STRESS

Logosoma Brain Training is a four-step process that liberates your brain from the stresses that can derail your clear thinking. Stress can impair ordinary mental, emotional, and behavioral functioning. Chronic stress can produce inappropriate patterns of avoidance, confrontation, or paralysis. The stress of everyday life is only part of the problem. In fact, your brain has an enemy within, which I call phantom stress. Phantom

13

stress is triggered by nonconscious stress memories, rooted in adverse experiences from childhood or your earlier adult life. This book will teach you how to track down and neutralize the toxic effects from past stress that created the phantom stress in your brain. These associations from the past eclipse appropriate emotional responses to your life and derail healthy self-awareness, secure identity boundaries, and strong emotional connections.

In order to survive life's ups and downs, evolution has hard-wired us with a stress response system called the *allostatic mechanism*. Miraculous and complex in its design, it gives your body the ability to react to changes in the environment. When mobilized, we either fight or flee from a serious threat, much like our prehistoric ancestors when confronted by a predator. The stress response system performs this task by regulating hormones like cortisol and adrenaline, which can give us superhuman strength when faced with danger or help us wake up from a good night's sleep.

The evolution of the human nervous system has not kept up with the stresses that we have created for ourselves with the progress of civilization. The brain needs new skills to cope with the twenty-first century. So when external stresses of modern life become too great, as in the example above, they can overwhelm the allostatic system. When the system is chronically overloaded, you develop a condition called *allostatic load*. Dangerously high levels of stress hormones build up in the body, resulting in chronic stress.

The real enemy of your physical, mental, and social health, chronic stress is a silent killer. It can suppress and then damage your immune system. It can overwhelm your mental and emotional balance. Chronic stress will seriously impair your efforts to adapt to the challenges of everyday life, causing frustration, helplessness, and confusion to flourish. You begin to view yourself as a hostage: of your job, of your life circumstances, of your family and even of your children. The long list of medical ailments it can cause is alarming: coronary artery disease, obesity, hypertension, irritable bowel syndrome, melancholic depression, diabetes, insomnia, anorexia nervosa, alcoholism, panic disorder, drug addiction, obsessive-compulsive disorder, chronic fatigue syndrome, fibromyalgia, and neuronal brain damage, to name a few.

Phantom stress directly contributes to the toxic effects of chronic stress. Insidious and invisible, this deadly enemy appears unbidden, often triggered by the most seemingly trivial circumstances. When unleashed, it can cause destructive behavior and derail your ability to focus and think clearly. It thrives on worries about the future. Triggered by events as banal as a traffic jam, phantom stress causes an inappropriate emotional response in the present, like the internal suffering conversation of the driver above. Unless it is unmasked, it will undo your authentic sense of self, your relationships, and your potential for spiritual awakening.

LOGOSOMA BRAIN TRAINING: INTEGRATING EAST AND WEST

As a practicing clinician for more than twenty-five years, I have paid close attention to the full spectrum of interacting systems that make up a human being, from molecular biology to social connections. In the mid-1980s, I developed Logosoma Brain Training (LBT), integrating principles from modern neuroscience, psychotherapy, and the ancient practice of meditation. Learning principles of these reflective traditions helps you to attain what I call *mindful awareness*. Mindful awareness integrates the healthy reframing of your negative feelings with the ability to observe your mind without stress. Using both Eastern and Western reflective tools derived from meditation and psychotherapy, you will learn to solve old problems in new ways. Your brain can actually rewire its synaptic circuits, a process that neuroscience calls neuroplasticity. The mechanism of learning, neuroplasticity is enhanced by strong emotional experiences and focused attentional techniques. These skills hold the promise of actually rewiring your brain's stress response circuitry. Logosoma Brain Training guides you to create new neural connections in your brain. These new synaptic circuits will help you to say no to stress triggers in the future. Out of the grip of your phantom past, you can reconnect with your true self and all those people, places, and things that you love in the present.

I developed the term *logosoma* to designate the balanced integration of brain functions: cognition, emotion, and motivation. *Logosoma* is derived from two Greek terms: *logos* meaning "word" or "story," and *soma* meaning "body." I look at a human being as a *body* living in a *life story*, the narrative we create about ourselves in the world. The body is the physical side of the self, and the life story is the abstract side created by the brain. The body and story are continuously interacting and influencing each other, for better or worse.

OPTIMAL ADAPTIVE RESILIENCE

Emerging scientific evidence reveals that the stories you generate about yourself and your attachments—particularly to other people—have a profound effect on your health. *The body follows the story.* One key element of resilience to chronic stress is developing a personal story of *connectedness* with oneself and others. While Western science is only just beginning to unravel the molecular sociology of human relationships, ancient Eastern traditions such as Buddhist meditation and mind training have become great sources of wisdom, helping scientists better understand the complex relationship between mind and body.

Buddhist meditation training played an important role in my life during medical school. In 1976, I spent the summer studying medicine, meditation, and culture at the Tibetan Medical Center in Dharamsala, India, home of the exiled Dalai Lama of Tibet. Part of the curriculum involved meditation training and study of Buddha's *four noble truths*.

The first truth establishes the problem: life is suffering. The second truth identifies the cause: suffering arises from attachment. The third truth offers the solution: the cessation of suffering is possible by embracing the impermanence of all life experience. And the fourth truth details the method of implementing the solution: the path to avoid suffering in the future can be learned and practiced by following the eightfold path.

A few years later, when I was a trainee in child psychiatry in the early 1980s, I made a crucial link between Buddha's four noble truths and attachment theory, and Dr. John Bowlby's key lectures on the forming and breaking of relationships. Bowlby described the essential first step in successful adaptation to life as one of *secure attachment* between caregiver and infant. Recent developmental neuroscience is revealing how the successful interaction between infant and caregivers prepares the infant's brain for successful adaptation to stress in the future. Likewise, overwhelming or chronic stress can lead to insecure attachment during early development, predisposing the brain to stress and poor adaptation in the future.

Logosoma Brain Training helps you gain an increased awareness of the stress circuits in your brain that produce destructive emotions and behaviors. No matter what stressful history your brain has endured, your brain's neuroplasticity allows you to learn and practice new ways of adapting to your life in the present. You can transform the feelings of "just surviving" to "thriving and well being." **You have the ability to change your attitude and behaviors through Logosoma Brain Training**.

PART I

PHANTOM STRESS

Chapter 1

THE ENEMY WITHIN—MEET PHANTOM STRESS

Love dares you to change our way of caring about ourselves . . .
This is ourselves under pressure.
—**David Bowie/ Freddie Mercury**

JULES: THE SOUND OF BREAKING GLASS

Jules watched himself in disbelief as his fist flew toward the head of the person he loved most in the world, his wife Jane. In the millisecond before impact, it was only the last thread of conscious will that helped him divert the aim of his menacing blow. Grazing the head of his terrified wife, his fist hit the door window above her head. Jules heard his howling voice combine with the sound of shattering glass, the broken shards slashing his skin. But he felt no pain. His bloody fingers had gone numb. His heart was pounding in his chest. His ears were ringing with alarm. In shock, he felt as if he were in a dream or watching a movie.

Jane was the love of his life, the woman he wanted for the long haul. Wanting to marry and stay married, Jules spent some time in individual therapy and premarital couple work before he and Jane tied the knot. It was not easy, but Jules was determined to make it work.

Jules was really looking forward to having dinner with Jane. Having spent another long, stressful day setting up his new office, he was tired. But seeing Jane always put him in a randy mood. "How's the sexiest chef in town?" he asked. She teased him back while trying to pay attention to what she was cooking. As Jules moved in behind her for a tender snuggle, Jane took him by surprise. Her inviting and flirtatious voice became a stern, rejecting reprimand: "Can't you wait until after dinner!" Her body stiffened against his caress. Before Jules could utter a word, he felt a sudden surge of rage take his body hostage. His shoulders squared, as if readying for a battle.

What happened next left Jules in shock and Jane cowering with terror.

THE PROBLEM: CRIMES OF PASSION AND PHANTOM STRESS

The powerful and destructive emotions triggering Jules to swing impulsively at Jane emerge in people everywhere. Stress can overwhelm and derail your rational thinking, trigger destructive behavior, and sabotage your relationships. You may never be as violent or extreme as Jules, but I am sure you have experienced moments of impulsively screaming at a loved one, then felt the need to withdraw suddenly or else you would explode. And how many of us have stonewalled, when you suddenly go silent, and beam a look of contempt at those you want to talk to the most. All of these "ordinary" stress reactions may be triggered by today's up and downs. But they become amplified and destructive when charged by potent phantom stressors from the past, imprinted in your brain long before you can remember or accumulated over you adult life experience. Jules's workday stress and excitement at the prospect of seeing Jane clearly ratcheted up his adrenaline, but it did not trigger the violence. His frightening response did not come from the day's events, but from his own past. Buried deep within his nonconscious brain, Jules's chronic stress experienced during his childhood relationship with his mother and father laid the groundwork for his volatile temper.

The facts are in. The latest scientific evidence suggests the long reach of childhood stress on adult life can be devastating. Nonconscious stress from the past can trigger a full-blown stress reaction in the present. Meet phantom stress!

The sanctuary of healthy social bonds provides powerful protection from the stresses of everyday life. From childhood onwards, a secure tie with family, friends, and others helps your brain recover from stressful events. The stress load on your body and brain is lightened when you communicate stressful experiences with others.

Phantom stress is the enemy of *social connectedness*. As stress arises from invisible, nonconscious triggers, it is difficult to explain. The stress reaction appears irrational to the onlooker and feels mysterious to the hijacked brain. Phantom stress plays a key role in the development of the insidious killer, chronic stress. But unlike the daily stress that wears you down from the outside, phantom stress attacks indirectly from within, triggered by any circumstance recalling a fragment of a past stress.

Much like a lingering phantom limb, the illusion of sensation felt long after the amputation of a leg or hand, phantom stress feels real in the present, but was born in the past. It is a force that is so powerful it can make you needlessly suffer, fight, or run away from your loved ones as if your life depended on it. Left unchecked, it will tear the fabric of your social connectedness and be the undoing of the sanctuary of intimate relationships protecting you from the ravages of chronic stress.

Phantom stress can be activated simply, by a disapproving expression on your partner's face, a clipped response, a snub, being criticized or yelled at, manipulated, disrespected, or ignored. But it can also emerge from more complex repetitive situations—from a feeling of being deprived of something you need (sex, affection, or validation) to the pressure of accommodating the needs of others. Loss of control, for example, having to defer to a stronger personality like a domineering parent, partner, or boss, can cause the onslaught of phantom stress.

Memories of childhood relationships can cause phantom stress. Neglected or abused children often grow up and relive their painful memories in adult life. Yet, childhood memories are only one piece of this potent force. An old hurt or grudge from the recent past can trigger it as well, for example, an event in your adult life that happened last week, last month or ten years ago. Disasters both natural and man-made—the attack on the Word Trade Center on September 11, 2001, Hurricane Katrina, an earthquake, a tornado, a fire or car accident—can take on a life of their own. Traumatic events of the past can live on inside you, creating havoc in yourself and your relationship to those around you. Your phantom history is mapped unconsciously into your brain. You are left with the feelings, smells, and fragmentary glimpses of past stress.

Residing inside us all like a wicked double, phantom stress is a far more potent force than daily stressors like your job, the traffic, or the kids. And when it is awakened, all bets are off. Insidious and invisible, phantom stress appears unbidden, triggered by circumstances in the present or worries about the future. If left unmasked, it will play a critical role in the undoing of your authentic sense of self, your relationships, healthy physical habits, and your livelihood. Phantom stress derails clear thinking, triggers impulsive and destructive behaviors, and strips pleasure and intimacy from your relationships, if not your whole life. Phantom stress is truly the enemy within.

Let us be clear. Although it may be triggered by certain situations, events, and memories, phantom stress is just that—a *phantom*. Nothing is happening in the reality of the moment except a body memory. Like a phantom limb, it is residual stress, a *déjà vu* situation, a ghost of the past etched in the circuits of the brain rearing its head yet again, filling your body with fear or frustration. We all suffer the effects of phantom stress to varying degrees, but rarely recognize when it emerges from the subterranean memory bank in our brains.

THE CAUSE OF THE PROBLEM

Life is stressful. We feel the strain from the trauma of childbirth to each developmental hurdle of childhood. It continues into the formative years of adolescence, into early adulthood, until the end of the life cycle. Your stress response system, what scientists call the allostatic system, is miraculous and complex in its design. It is actually bolstered by each successful adaptation to life stress. During acute conditions, stress protects us; when chronically activated, it can actually do damage and accelerate disease.

We are still learning to adapt to the stresses of modern life, to overcrowded cities, to advertising techniques that promote status anxiety, to fluctuating mortgage rates, to world terrorism, or to planetary pollution. We need to adapt and to develop new, special skills in order to find personal and social balance to survive the challenges of the twenty-first century.

When phantom stress repeatedly distracts you from your efforts to adapt to the stresses of everyday life, you are on the verge of chronic stress. Feelings of frustration, helplessness and confusion grow. If your body is gradually overwhelmed by dysfunction of your allostatic system, you begin to view yourself as a hostage—of your job, of your life circumstances, of your family, and even of your children.

BRAIN SCAN: PHANTOM STRESS AND INNOCENT BYSTANDERS

Do you remember your childhood home? Now try to recall a specific place in the house where you experienced intense fear, for example, walking down the creaky stairs into a dank, dark cellar when you were two. If you return to that house today, you might feel nervous or edgy when nearing the staircase, but you would most likely not remember why. You could even go to a different house with a similar staircase and have the same jittery feeling. Your breathing might become shallow, your neck muscles might tighten, or your stomach might flip-flop in anticipation of the old fear. The source of this powerful negative emotion was registered at an age when you were too young to form a conscious, retrievable memory.

Scientists now know there is nothing hard-wired into your brain's basic makeup to make you frightened of staircases. It is your life experience that has made your brain associate such staircases with the fear you felt as a child. There is nothing inherently scary about the staircase itself. It is an innocent bystander. It is your brain that causes you to feel the fear. It triggers a stress response without you really knowing why.

THE SOLUTION: LOGOSOMA BRAIN TRAINING

As a psychiatric clinician with twenty-five years of experience, I have learned to pay attention to the full spectrum of interacting systems from the molecular level up to the social connections. In the mid-1980s, I developed Logosoma Brain Training for my patients. It is my proprietary method for evaluating and training the brain to integrate the two most basic aspects of being: the body (*soma*) and the world of words (*logos*).

A human being is a body living in a life story, the self-generated narrative we create about ourselves in the world. The body and the life story are continuously interacting for better or for worse. Emerging scientific evidence reveals that the attitude you hold about your physical and emotional self, the stories you think and speak about your health, and your relationships and your behavior profoundly influence your adaptability to stress. The body follows the story.

Your attachments form the heart of your personal story. Healthy attachment to your body, to others, to things, activities, places, and even your own memories are all keys to social connectedness, the essence of resilience to chronic stress. Although Western science is only just beginning to unravel the molecular sociology of human relationships, the wisdom of the ancient East provides specific brain practices that can amplify our scientific discoveries to wage the war with chronic stress.

ANCIENT WISDOM AND MODERN SCIENCE: FROM BUDDHA TO BOWLBY TO BRAIN STRESS

During medical school, I spent a summer studying at the Tibetan Medical Center in Dharamsala, India, home of the exiled Dalai Lama of Tibet. During my meditation training, I discovered the roots of my Logosoma Brain Training, in the four noble truths of the Buddha. The first truth, "Life is suffering," addresses the problem. The second truth identifies that "the cause of suffering arises from attachment." The third truth gives the solution, namely to "embrace the impermanence of all life experience," and the fourth truth offers a method to implement the solution in the eightfold path.

As a trainee in child psychiatry in the early 1980s, I found John Bowlby's attachment theory to have a special resonance with the Buddha's wisdom. Bowlby described the essential first step in successful adaptation to life as one of secure attachment between caregiver and infant. Recent developmental neuroscience is discovering how the successful interaction between infant and caregiver prepares and protects the infant's brain for adaptation to stress in the future. Conversely, overwhelming or chronic stress can lead to insecure attachment during early development, predisposing the brain to vulnerability and poor adaptation to stress in the future.

In my study and practice of ancient meditation, contemporary developmental psychology, and neuroscience, I realized that the skills needed to promote a healthy sense of self, resilience to the stresses of everyday life, secure emotional relationships, and successful creative adaptation to an ever-changing world *can be learned*. No matter what damage the traumatic past may have caused, you have the ability to change your attitude and behaviors through effortful mental training. By changing the way you focus on stress triggers, you can actually rewire the way your brain deals with the stress-driven impulses to fight and flee. Neutralizing the destructive effects of phantom stress will prevent the development of chronic stress, creating the clearing for you to form new secure relationships with yourself and others.

Reframing the Buddha's wisdom with Bowlby's attachment theory and the neuroscience of stress, we might say in modern scientific terms that:

Life is stressful.

The cause of stress is disconnection from secure attachment.

The cessation of stress begins with the refocusing of attention.

The path to secure attachment is to embrace impermanence and reconnect.

THE METHOD: FOUR STEPS TO CHANGING YOUR BRAIN

Logosoma Brain Training is four-step process that liberates your brain from the stressors that cause self-sabotaging patterns of thought, emotion, and behavior. These nonconscious phantom stressors are rooted in adverse childhood experiences or past stresses from your adult life. I will teach you to track down and neutralize the toxic effects from the past associations that created the phantom stress in your brain. These associations from the past eclipse appropriate emotional responses in the present.

Phantom stress derails healthy self-awareness, secure identity boundaries, and strong emotional bonds. I will teach you a new awareness of the stress circuits in your brain that produce destructive emotions and behaviors.

Logosoma Brain Training combines focused attention techniques borrowed from the ancient Eastern practice of meditation with a Western approach of giving reflective attention to emotional memories from modern psychotherapy. With practice, the training will provide you with objective views of old patterns of self-sabotaging behaviors and thought patterns that impair your personal life, your relationships, and your career. Cultivating reflective attention to emotional memories empowers you to neutralize the toxic effects of phantom stress. By liberating yourself from the stuck patterns of chronic stress, your brain can create new brain circuits to solve old emotional problems. These new solutions form the foundation for new self-respecting habits and open the way for you to develop lasting emotional connectedness with everything around you.

Logosoma Brain Training encourages the use of language to reframe the physical and emotional stresses of your life. Using words to reframe your pain and your negative emotion empowers you to turn destructive urges into meaningful communication. Your new life story, grounded in compassion and honesty, will lead your body out of the stuck physiology of chronic stress.

As you start practicing Logosoma Brain Training, you begin to objectify the enemy within—phantom stress. The four-step process will show you how to:

1. *Refuse* stress triggers
2. *Refocus* your attention to down-regulate from stress triggers
3. *Reflect* to connect with your authentic self
4. *Reconnect* with your relationships

Over time, as you practice the Logosoma Brain Training, you will develop a clearer sense of personal meaning, a deeper sense of emotional security within yourself and with your relationships, and more creative forms of resilience to the stress of everyday life.

Brain Scan: The Birth of Phantom Stress

What exactly triggers the birth of phantom stress?

Let us start with the most critical activity of all living creatures, survival. Like all other mammals, we have developed a sophisticated survival mechanism: the five Fs—freeze, fight, flight, feed, and fornicate. The five Fs provide our body with the mechanism to adapt to changes in the environment by increasing the heart rate, becoming hyperfocused on danger or mating, and increasing respiration. We make critical choices in distinguishing mates from predators, food from toxins, and friend from foe. This learning system has a two-lane highway for collecting important information: the *implicit* memory system designed to record important data in a nonconscious manner through experience (learning to swim or throw a spear), and the *explicit* memory system, requiring conscious effort to store information that can be retrieved through conscious effort (learning to read and write).

If you conjure up a charged experience, a *memory of emotion*, you are activating your explicit memory system, stored in the left side of the brain where language and rational thinking are processed. These memories, such as your first kiss, your wedding day, or the birth of a baby are readily available to your consciousness. They can be retrieved and pondered, like pictures in the family photo album, but do not necessarily activate the body's emotional responses at the same magnitude of the original experience.

By contrast, *emotional memories* are part of your implicit memory system, stored largely in the right brain. They operate outside of awareness. Implicit memory is thought to encode critical aspects of experience that have not been symbolized, such as actions (skills and habits), perceptions, sensations, and emotional states. Emotional memories activate the body's freeze, fight, and flight physiology; it feels just like the stressful event is happening all over again. Conscious awareness is unnecessary to trigger an emotional memory, although the responses to these memories—the feelings, hyper arousal, sensations, images and urges to act—can be known consciously. When an emotional memory cascades into actual behaviors, you have just been visited by phantom stress.

Infancy and early childhood are a breeding ground for *emotional memories*. When a child's developing brain adapts to overwhelming or chronic stress by pushing it out of awareness, denying there is a problem, and pretending that everything is OK (as children often do), a *phantom stressor* is born. Although erasing the source of stress brings a feeling of safety, all that has really happened is the stress is now invisible to the child's conscious awareness. Its brain circuits still hold traces of the stress, hidden within the neural network, silently stored as nonconscious *emotional memories*, waiting to be triggered.

JULES'S BACK STORY: PHANTOM STRESS AND MISTAKEN IDENTITY

"I didn't know where the anger and urge to hit her came from," Jules confessed.

No one knows what a phantom stressor is until it has an effect. Phantom stress can be triggered by almost anything, often a fragmentary memory of a past stress. For Jules, Jane's sudden emotional withdrawal startled him, awakening a knee-jerk behavior that he had developed as a teenager. "Hit first and ask questions later." Jules lamented, "I spent years in therapy changing my macho attitude with women. I find it hard to believe that it can come back without warning, causing me to almost hit the lady I love!"

"I spent most of my childhood with my controlling and critical mother," Jules recalled. "I'm a younger twin. My brother Joel and I were never that close. My parents' marriage lasted all of three years before my dad, a professional athlete, went off with some cheerleader. He managed to get custody of my brother when he left. He always favored him. Mom adored my brother too, but I was the 'good listener,' the one mom turned to when she wanted to vent her anger toward dad. The only way I got her attention was to listen to her complain about dad. She never really seemed to be interested in listening to me otherwise.

"My father always treated me as a loser because of my size. I was shorter than my brother. Dad was almost never home. God, I really wanted his approval! But he only called me names like wimp or crybaby. I hated him for it. And I think I became this sort of macho guy, always looking for a fight, to give myself a kind of armor against heartbreak."

Jules spent years in therapy. The experience certainly helped improve his emotional intelligence but he still had not mastered control of his impulsive anger. When we connected his childhood stress patterns to his attachments with both mother and father, Jules declared, "Holy smokes! When Jane stiffened up and rejected my bid for affection, I must have been triggered! I mistook her for my mother and my father, for every time they rejected my overtures for affection, and started swinging at Jane!"

In Jules's brain, the phantom stress circuits shaped by his chronic disappointments with both his parents had laid the foundation for his angry, often violent, response to disconnection and rejection. Throwing a punch at Jane was a case of phantom stress as *mistaken identity*.

Anyone can be triggered into feeling the same intense shame, rejection, envy, or jealousy we felt during childhood. When your brain becomes flooded with too much adrenaline, these childlike feelings can drive you to act impulsively. While you may not have acted as extremely as punching a window in a fit of anger, you certainly may have felt like that way at one time or another.

STOP! Refuse, Refocus, and Reflect on Your Feelings Now

Knowing he was in trouble, Jules was eager to take instructions at the beginning of his Logosoma Brain Training on how to redirect his attention.

"I'm in trouble, Dr. Romero," Jules began. "When I met Jane, we had this great connection. I do love her. But ever since that meltdown in the kitchen, I hate myself. I'm so ashamed of what I did. It was so stupid! I should be able to control my anger. I'm an adult . . ."

"Stop!" I said. "I want you to tell me how you're feeling right now."

"Like an idiot," he declared.

"Jules, I asked you how you are feeling right now, not what your opinion of yourself is."

Jules took a long pause and softly whispered, "I'm not sure . . . maybe frustrated? I also feel scared, but even worse, I feel helpless. It really scares me to feel helpless. I can never get Jane's attention. And that makes me feel impotent, like a failure. I'm afraid she'll leave."

I validated his emotional answer with the following coaching, "Okay, that's good Jules. You've just refocused your attention on your emotional state and identified your feelings. This is the beginning of healing. Name your feelings. Own your feelings! The adrenaline rushing through your brain has triggered a fight/flight response. And unless you refocus, you won't be able to think about the damage you're doing to yourself, your partner, and your partnership."

With lots of practice on his own, Jules was able to learn to say "Stop!" when he felt his body being triggered. He learned to identify the tell-tale bodily symptoms—the butterflies in his stomach, a tense neck, a surge of fear, or rising anger—as signs of high levels of stress hormones. This is the first step in Logosoma Brain Training: *refuse the stress invitation*.

After identifying his body's response to being triggered, Jules could begin to refocus his attention away from the trigger to regulate the cascade of the stress hormones driving his fight/flight response, shutting down his ability to think clearly. With practice, Jules learned to give himself time to "chill out," taking up to half an hour to regulate his activated stress system. Thereafter, he learned to take time to reflect on what actually happened *before* he tried to discuss it with anyone, particularly Jane.

BRAIN SCAN: WORRY, RE-REMEMBERING, AND THE GROWTH OF PHANTOM STRESS

Phantom stress can occur at any time. A worry about a stress from last week can trigger remembering the episode. It can hit us again next week or a year from now. And each time a stressful incident is re-remembered, the worry adds a new memory in your brain. The worry memory goes through a process of being reloaded, reaccumulated, and re-remembered in a slightly different form, what neuroscientists call the *reconsolidation of memory*. When a negative emotional memory is reconsolidated nonconsciously, particularly during stressful moments, its charge dramatically increases.

Before Jules began his Logosoma Brain Training, he ruminated on negative memories of his critical father and controlling, needy mother. Every time he worried, he triggered another reconsolidation of a negative emotional memory, fueling the growth of his resentments toward his parents. In the re-remembering of stressful events, the meaning became more progressively mired in negative feeling. So you can see how Jules's childhood wired him to explode when he was disappointed by his most intimate emotional relationships.

BRAIN SCAN: FALSE MAPS OF EMOTION

Neuroscientists have recently discovered that emotions start as physical reactions to outside stimulus from the environment or from within the brain. Your body tracks stimuli from the outside world through your five senses. Registered as sensations, they are stored in the brain as neural maps of the body state for future reference. For example, when you are sitting in a comfortable chair, your sense of touch will send a message from your skin to your brain telling you it is all right to relax. Conversely, it will alert you if you just sat on a tack. Two areas of the brain, the somatosensory cortex and the insula, record and interpret your sensory data into higher levels of conscious awareness. When you become consciously aware of sensations, transforming them into conscious images, you can identify them as feelings.

Recent brain-imaging techniques show the same areas of the brain that map body states are also activated or deactivated by strong feelings. When test subjects were asked to concentrate on memories of intense feelings (happiness, sadness, anger, or fear), the somatosensory cortex and the insula respond as if there were an outside stimulus. In laboratory tests, when subjects reported their intense feelings, a spike in skin electrical activity occurred. This indicates that the awareness of what you "feel" is always preceded by a nonconscious emotional surge in the neural body maps. Neuroscientists now believe that emotions are actually nonconscious body states that precede the conscious awareness of feelings.

Most negative emotions are first recorded nonconsciously as neural maps of body states in the brain before they ever become conscious as negative feelings. Outside stimuli tracked by your senses move up the central nervous system to the brain—hence their name, bottom-up messages—eventually making their way to an area involved in thinking, the prefrontal cortex (PFC). As your body sends moment-by-moment signals upward to the brain, the somatosensory cortex constructs the neural body maps you will use to cross-reference and interpret the state of the body in the future, helping you to answer questions like "Am I safe? Am I in danger? Does he like me?" However, there can be wrinkles in this system. Maps constructed during stressful times in the past, tattooed in the brain by the stress hormones and blurred from consciousness, can be triggered and misperceived as "here and now" events. These false maps of the body's present state can interrupt the accurate assessment of what is going on in the present. These false maps are the breeding ground in the brain for phantom stressors.

Phantom stressors can hijack your clear-thinking PFC with false signals that lead to inappropriate freeze/fight/flight behavior. Your PFC is activated by happiness and deactivated by the sadness condition. We all know how a down mood can cause mental sluggishness or how an up mood can stimulate a flow of positive thoughts. Knowing how your brain works can help you accept that it is not your personality, your past, your parents, or even your partner that disrupts your intimacy. While the stress response is a natural phenomenon helping us identify threats and avoid danger, it can also distort your perception of those you value and love. Knowing how your brain creates phantom stress empowers Logosoma Brain Training.

PHANTOM STRESS—A STORY IN THE BODY

Nature designed your right brain to remember emotionally painful and frightening incidents. Your very survival depends on it. Good or bad, these incidents happen in the body and become scripted in your brain. They become part of a story, your story. The fact that you cannot see the stories or the stress does not make either any less real. When a past stress is triggered by a reminder in the present, you may react with a private assessment that is more rooted in the past than what is happening now. This can lead to inappropriate reactions. For example, if your friend comments on your hair being wind-blown in a joking manner, you may respond defensively in the same way you did as a teenager when your mother made the same comment in a similar tone of voice.

Long before phantom stress gets you or your relationships get into trouble, you can learn to identify what I call "stress conversations." A stress conversation can be a private narrative in your head or an actual conversation with someone. These conversations inappropriately trigger your allostatic system. You find yourself feeling defensive, argumentative or frozen as a result of the stress hormones flooding your brain. Stress conversations are triggered by the stress of everyday life and, more importantly, by the phantom stressors etched into your brain from adverse emotionally charged childhood experiences, recent grudges, frustrations, or from a singular traumatic event.

Phantom stress flourishes in an atmosphere of secrecy, avoidance, and emotional distance. Secrecy is a story of suppressed emotion. Suppressing emotions has been demonstrated to amplify and prolong normal stress response. The longer a suppressed emotion is avoided, the greater the stress reaction becomes. This ongoing cover-up of emotion allows a threatening story in the body to grow and to expand. Ultimately, the fear of discovery strips us of our want and need for intimacy, leaving us isolated and alone.

THE BREEDING GROUND FOR PHANTOM STRESS

Isolation, self-pity, and self-criticism are the best friends of phantom stress. It feeds on distance and anger from others, and is nourished through silence and pretence.

"Before I started therapy and learned to reflect on my feelings, I would just stuff my anger or hurt. I didn't want to look like a whiner or a sissy," Jules recalled.

I explained to Jules that the cost of that suppressed emotion was an increase in his stress load.

When you withdraw from your social connections and hold your stress inside, the stress load actually worsens. The suppressed emotion kindles more negative emotional thoughts that become obsessive ruminations. Repeatedly visiting the stress in your mind with worry triggers again your stress physiology, escalating the stress hormones and creating a muddled state of thinking. When you worry, holding your stress silently inside, your phantom stressors are gaining ground.

What is your phantom stressors made of? Emotional memories, nonconscious body maps, and a hair-trigger stress reaction can all combine to activate your catastrophic imagination. Your brain makes up stories to explain the frightening unknown and to soothe you in times that are scary and unwieldy. So it is natural for you to blame others for your troubles. Those closest to you act as an easy screen for your phantom projections. Logosoma Brain Training empowers you to take charge of your own history, your own pain and fears. Connectedness springs from an integrated relationship between the body and the body's life story. I will teach you how to listen to your own life story and to the stories of your relationships. Listening is the secret to regaining your connection with yourself and the key to successful human relationships.

As you have now seen, the enemy may not be your partner, your boss, or your demanding child. The enemy may be within—phantom stress! The good news is that phantom stress can be unmasked, navigated, and even neutralized. And this book will teach you how.

QUIET MOMENTS OF REFLECTION

We have come to the end of chapter 1, The Enemy Within—Meet Phantom Stress. To help you to remember all that you have learned here, a short review is provided below. The review is part of a continuing commitment you are making to yourself.

1. I know that my body's survival mechanism, freeze, fight, and flight, can become overwhelmed with chronic stress.
2. I accept that stressful events in my past can be stored in my brain maps without my awareness.
3. I accept that the brain map of past stressors can be triggered in the present, and emotional memories from the past can distort my perception and activate inappropriate, full-blown survival reactions.
4. I declare that I want to learn and practice new ways to manage my intense emotions and redirect my self-sabotaging behavior.

Chapter 2

THE END OF CONNECTEDNESS: FROM PHANTOM STRESS TO CHRONIC STRESS

In my beginning is my end.

—T. S. Eliot

It is a cool evening in the spring of 2002, and the normally empty entry hall of the New York Academy of Sciences is stifling hot and packed with anxious visitors. The crowd is jostling for seats in the academy's small lecture hall, housed in the stately Woolworth Mansion on East Sixty-third Street in Manhattan. Tonight's speaker is the eminent Dr. Bruce McEwen, head of the Harold and Margaret Milliken Hatch Laboratory of Neuroendocrinology at Rockcfcller University in New York City. The topic causing the clamor is *The End of Stress as We Know It*, McEwen's groundbreaking book on stress, an original take on how the brain influences our glands and immune system. A wide range of ethnic and socioeconomic groups from ages eighteen to eighty populate the noisy hall. There is a sudden hush as McEwen takes the podium and asked, "How many of you have ever considered yourself 'stressed out'? Please raise your hand." As McEwen takes the lead by raising his own first, the audience is quickly transformed into a sea of waving hands, launching an evening exploring the word *stress*, the ancient survival mechanism of freeze/fight/flight, a signal for danger, a mirror of our modern life.

What is stressful for one may not be stressful for another. For some of us, stress can be experienced as a disturbing relationship with our family, job, or balancing the checkbook. For others, it can be a bodily discomfort, a churning stomach, sweaty palms, a racing heart, tense muscles, sleepless nights, or worried thoughts. Whatever the symptoms, you know one thing is certain—stress is the name of your enemy. Although this enemy has external triggers, it can invade your body. And when stressors take up residence, when they become chronic visitors, they can take your body and brain hostage and destroy your health and most intimate relationships.

STRESSED OUT: MORE THAN JUST A FEELING

The real enemy of your physical, emotional, mental, and social health is *chronic stress*. It damages your body and triggers worries that can overwhelm your mental and emotional balance. Both the physical and emotional symptoms spring from the same chemical root. McEwen identifies the toxic agents of stress to be altered levels of the stress hormone, cortisol, and the production of toxic proteins called inflammatory cytokines. Single episodes of stress do not have the power to alter the normal flow of cortisol or the overproduction of cytokines. When your allostatic system is working well, cortisol is actually a miracle hormone, helping you adjust to react to the stresses of everyday life and then calm down.

But when your *allostatic system* is constantly in the "on" position, triggered over and over, cortisol levels become elevated or reduced. Cytokines can interfere with the immune system's response to stress, causing a variety of mental and physical disorders, especially depression and illness. By throwing the normal function of the *allostatic system* into dysfunction, your body cannot relax. You begin to develop *allostatic load*. The list of medical conditions resulting from the allostatic load of chronic stress is long and scary: coronary artery disease, obesity, hypertension, irritable bowel syndrome, melancholic depression, diabetes, insomnia, anorexia nervosa, alcoholism, panic disorder, drug addiction, obsessive-compulsive disorder, chronic fatigue syndrome, fibromyalgia, neuronal brain damage, and more. The social consequences are just as daunting: social avoidance, divorce, child abuse, absenteeism from work, job loss, passive-aggressive behaviors, to mention a few.

Chronic stress during childhood is perhaps the most devastating enemy of healthy development and adaptive resilience to stress later in adult life. McEwen and an international group of scientists are uncovering the fact that a child's developing brain is even more susceptible to stress than the fully developed adult brain. In fact, the allostatic system is more or less shaped by the quality of your early attachments during infancy.

As a practicing clinical child and family psychiatrist for twenty-five years, I have witnessed the devastating consequences of adverse childhood experiences on individuals and families. Identity development, secure relationships, healthy physical development, authentic aspirations in your career, and even the choice of where you live are all strongly affected by your ability to adapt and become resilient to the stresses of everyday life. Surveying 17,000 members of the *Kaiser Permanente Health Plan* in the San Diego area, stress researcher Vincent Felitti's *Adverse Childhood Experiences* study discovered that adverse childhood experience, not exposure to drugs or drug dealers, played a key role in determining which children would become addicted to drugs or alcohol in their adult lives.

THE MOLECULAR SOCIOLOGY OF STRESS

The development of healthy emotional connections is extremely vulnerable to the shadow of childhood stressors. Your ability to resist being trigged by your stressors, or what I call optimal adaptive resilience (OAR), will profoundly affect the spectrum of core relationships, for example with your body, your sense of self, your partner, family, friends, and your career. The mechanisms of the long-lasting grip of stress are obviously much more complex than the simple production of stress hormones. Indeed, McEwen describes his research into stress and resilience as "molecular sociology." Successful adaptation to stress involves many complex systems. It starts at the molecular level within cells. It continues to the synaptic connections between the neurons in your brain, to the neural networks that mediate your emotions, thoughts and motivations, and to your social connectedness. These social synapses, where words and behaviors function like neurotransmitters, shape your relationships with others. When the bonds of your attachments are overwhelmed by perpetual stress and you feel like a hostage in chronically stressed social connections, the cascade of dysfunction ripples through your body, traveling right back down to the molecular world of DNA regulation.

What is even more unsettling is that your brain adapts to overwhelming or chronic stress by pushing it out of awareness, denying that it is a problem, pretending that everything is OK. Once your brain succeeds in erasing stress from consciousness, you feel safe. But all you have done is make the stress invisible to your awareness. And you have given birth to a phantom stressor! Your brain circuits will hold traces of the stress, hidden in its neural maps, silently stored as nonconscious emotional memories. But when you encounter some fragmentary reminder of the original situation that stressed you in the past, you can experience a full-blown stress reaction in the present. And the worst part is you are totally unaware of where this fear reaction comes from.

LYNN: MONEY CAN'T BUY YOU CONNECTEDNESS

When she came to see me, Lynn looked much younger than her years. A self-made woman with a thriving business, Lynn was a financial success story, yet she was frustrated. Despite her many personal attributes, she was unable to kindle a new love relationship since her divorce. Although there was no lack of suitors, their financial status seemed to be derailing Lynn from being able to make a genuine connection. "I'm so fed up with dating scene, I don't bother any more. I just stay at work all the time. I've met one loser after another. None of them make any real money compared to me. And when they do, they're married! I'm having trouble sleeping. I'm so irritable with people at work. I even lost my temper last week, for no good reason. I have stomach aches all the time. My internist says they're caused by stress. I'm even beginning to question my career," she complained.

"My marriage was blissful for the first three years," Lynn continued, "but I spent the fourth year constantly arguing about money with my husband. He called himself an entrepreneur. But I discovered that it was just a cover for being what he really was—a reckless gambler. All of his risky investments went wrong. He lost all of his money. And I wasn't about to spend my life bailing him out of his debt. So I left him."

BACK STORY: LYNN, MONEY AND FINANCIAL INSECURITY

Lynn had a major phantom in her closet. She had grown up with wealth and social status. Her financially successful father adored her socialite mother, a perfectionist in manner and appearance. Lynn and her sister idealized their parents. They seemed to embody the perfect marriage. The sisters had nannies and maids to take care of them. So it was easier for Lynn to focus on school and excel. Intending to take the family to a higher level of wealth, her father made some risky investments. They failed and the family almost lost everything. "It happened so fast. One day I was living in a mansion with maids and cooks, and the next I was in an ordinary house doing the dishes."

"I was only 14 when I watched my mother suffer the humiliation of dad's business failure," Lynn explained. "She resented him. She criticized him over and over. He started to drink, and the booze impaired any chance for him to recover his financial status. My world collapsed in a matter of weeks. I went numb and retreated into my studies. Dad died of alcoholic liver cirrhosis when I was in college. I had to borrow money and apply for assistance to finish my graduate degree. I vowed to myself that I would be a millionaire. And I'd never depend on a man for anything ever again."

Lynn's first husband was a young businessman fresh out of school with his MBA. She met him during graduate school. But the marriage was doomed to fail after Lynn got her degree and started to make more money than her husband. When she landed an executive position with a big financial firm on Wall Street, she separated from her husband. Without thinking or reflecting about her emotions, she filed for divorce and moved into her own apartment a month later. "It was a financial choice," she observed. "We started out so happy. Why didn't it last? Why couldn't we keep it together?"

Having heard the same questions from my patients for years, I know the number one enemy of relationships is not the stress of everyday life, but rather the stress within the relationship itself. A growing scientific literature has suggested that marital discord is a risk factor for illness and early death. In addition, depression and stress are associated with enhanced production of proinflammatory cytokines that influence a spectrum of conditions associated with aging, such as atherosclerosis and dementia.

BRAIN SCAN: THE STRESS CONNECTION WITH DISCONNECTION

Developmental neuroscience demonstrates that chronic stress can impair human relationships. In my clinical practice, I see how chronic stress is also gnawing at the very connectedness of my patients to their bodies, to themselves, to their families, to their careers, and to their community and culture. The potent mixture of everyday stress ignited by phantom stressors can fill your bloodstream with potent stress hormones, clouding your clear thinking and distorting your true emotions. In such emotionally charged states, your ability to stay tuned in to the moment is impaired. It is very easy for your attention to get disconnected from whatever you are doing through minor disappointments or misunderstandings.

Lynn recalls, "Once my ex and I started to drift apart over his attitude toward money, even the littlest things would trigger me. Why did he always have to buy the expensive bottled water? I hated it. He was bringing in less than a third of our household income. And I was quite happy with the cheaper water!"

Phantom stress triggers the behaviors and attitudes that make you vulnerable to chronic stress. Chronic stress is the toxin that can take your brain hostage and lead toward the end of connectedness.

JUST WHAT IS CONNECTEDNESS?

Human relationships form the core of connectedness. Social attachments, emotional bonds, physical intimacy, trusting relationships, and shared memories are all elements of connectedness. But I mean something more than just human relationships when I use the word connectedness. I also mean the emotional connection to your body, your life story, your sense of personal meaning, your career, and your environment. As individuals, as couples, as families, and as communities, human beings evolved to connect with each other. Being connected in all of these realms provides you with optimal adaptive resilience to the ravages of chronic stress.

Connectedness is complex. Insecure attachments produce chronic stress. Connections charged with negative emotion trigger destructive behaviors. Secret connections based on deceit can lead to self-sabotaging behaviors and addiction. Weak connections invite feelings of worthlessness and despair. Logosoma Brain Training aims to help you establish and maintain healthy, balanced, resilient connectedness in all of your relationships. Another word for positive emotional connectedness is *love*.

THE ARCHITECTURE OF HUMAN CONNECTIONS

Developmental attachment theory can be understood in terms of the relationship between an infant and its mother. Secure attachment emerges from a mother's attunement to her baby. Their connection reverberates through turn-taking interactions: the mother's adoring eyes beam into the eager gaze of her baby, the warmth of her hand touching the baby's skin provides a firm and flexible boundary, her reassuring fragrance envelops the baby during nursing. A mother's style of synchronized movement mirrors and validates her child's gestures. The music of a mother's voice can soothe her baby to sleep. The world of secure connections weaves emotions, sensations, and sounds together in an interactive tapestry. Connectedness is reciprocal, a creative interplay for both mother and baby. The stress circuitry in the baby's developing brain records the emotional experience in terms of attachment—shaped by countless repeated connections, disconnections, and reconnections—with the baby's mother. The textured journey for this infant-mother connection lays a foundation for all future connections the person will explore over the course of a lifetime.

Infant research has made it clear that *secure attachment is an experience essential to sustain human life*. A "good enough mother," one capable of establishing a secure attachment with her baby, is the launching pad for connectedness. Your sense of security with your body, with your identity, with your family and friends is rooted in this first connection to life. We dream of timeless connections. And when they vanish, we feel profound disappointment, deprived, done in, angry, and sometimes even helpless. We yearn to rekindle those early feelings, longing to recapture the connection.

The bond of love is created in a two-way process. Like a strong fabric, it is woven in the brains of mother-infant, husband-wife, or any lasting bond. The physical sensations, the feelings, the language, the actions, and the memories you experience in your relationships define your connections. Each of these threads of experience wires your brain's synaptic circuits and neural networks to create maps of experience in your brain. Balanced integration of these critical elements in your relationships will produce the connective tissue of all great lasting bonds.

As a child and family psychiatrist, I discovered early on how developmental and attachment theories focus on the way stress shapes all of your physical, emotional, psychological, and behavioral lives. Connectedness is one of the most important elements in developing optimal adaptive resilience to chronic stress, the number one enemy of connectedness. My clinical experience, combined with the most recent stress and marital research, supports the idea that nonconscious stressors from the past, which I call phantom stress, is the most toxic, invisible threat to long-lasting emotional bonds. I have spent the last thirty years tracking down this culprit and developing ways to neutralize its destructive force.

THE FOUR GUARDIANS OF SECURE ATTACHMENT: THE STORY OF WE

What will prevent your relationships from being taken hostage by chronic stress? Science clearly demonstrates that secure attachments protect us from the ravages of stress. So getting to know your phantom stressors is critical, along with keeping what I call the *four guardians* of secure attachment alive and engaged.

So what are the *four guardians*? When you look at individuals, couples, or families that appear to have something special in their relationships—no matter how long they've been together—you will notice that they exhibit the four crucial ingredients for successful intimacy:

- Physical contact (skinship)
- Emotional bonding
- Language—the shared narrative of "We"
- Memory—the neural network of lasting intimacy

These four elements are the foundations of secure connectedness. Taken together, they give rise to what I call the *Story of We*. The *four guardians* develop during childhood according to how our mothers and/ or fathers interacted with us. For better or for worse, we all bring our childhood experiences to our adult relationships. Let us take a closer look.

♥ **Physical contact, or skinship,** is the first element and describes the skin-to-skin relationship, such as the mother-child connection. I like the new shorthand word, skinship, created by Japanese popular language to designate the tactile world of intimacy. This is the realm of cuddles, coos, hugs, handholding, kisses, and sex. While you might think that adult sexuality dominates the world of physical closeness, the power of hugs and cuddles may play an even greater role in reducing stress in marriages and families.

♥ **Emotional bonds** spring from intensely shared emotional states. The secure and/or insecure attachments of childhood shape the complex neural circuitry for social attachments in adult life, especially intimate relationships. The power of emotional bonds cannot be overstated. They inspire feelings from the sublime to the abominable. And they can overwhelm rational judgment, moving people to extreme acts, such as those found in *Romeo and Juliet* or the front page of any tabloid.

♥ **Language** is the most human trait of connectedness. Imagine for a moment waking up one day unable to speak, read, or write. To approximate this experience, imagine a visit to a foreign country where you do not speak or read the language and have no friends. Pretty scary! Well, let me tell you a personal story.

While visiting Kyoto, I was separated from my touring group. And I will never forget the overwhelming anxiety of being lost. I had stayed too long at Sanju-Sangen-Do, a magnificent twelfth-thirteenth century Buddhist temple. In fact, I got lost in studying the unique faces of the one thousand golden Buddhas. Time just evaporated. Then I looked at my watch. I was late! I raced back to the hotel, but my group had already left for the train station. I grabbed my bags and hopped into a taxi. Not able to speak Japanese, I started mumbling and making signs with my hands, desperately trying to communicate "train station" to the driver. He grinned at me with no clue as to where I wanted to go. Then I remembered one critical Japanese word, Shinkansen, the name of the bullet train that runs between Tokyo and Kyoto. At last, he turned his meter on, and we drove away. My heart was racing, and my head spinning. "If I miss this train, I'll be lost forever in Kyoto," I continued to think. My body was overwhelmed with feelings of disconnection, as if I were alone on another planet. And just as suddenly as the fear had been triggered by my inability to communicate, it disappeared. I found an English-speaking attendant at the information booth and discovered that, no, my party had not abandoned me. I was able to reconnect with them. What a difference a word can make.

After my Kyoto experience, I knew for certain that language provides us with a sense of orientation, safety, security, and even identity. Without language, I had felt disconnected and helpless. It became very clear to me in Kyoto that the shared narrative of "We" is essential for the most basic necessities of life.

Language gives the human imagination the power of the word to create infinitely complex narratives emotionally charged with the color, texture, sound, taste, and smell that shape our relationships with partners, families, society, culture, and nature. In fact, even before you are born, your nervous system begins the miraculous work of synthesizing all the sensory experiences that you will eventually come to know as yourself. Language is so crucial to our survival that nature took special care to equip our brains with special cells. Called mirror neurons, they appear to be critical for developing the ability to create language.

♥ **Memory** is perhaps the most essential element of the *four guardians*. As the developing infant's brain records emotional experiences with its mother, learning important facts about the world, a miraculous process begins—the becoming of a human "self." Memory defines who you are by connecting you with your past. The meaning you derive from reflecting on your past gives you the potential for the resilience to stress. Meaning and reflection give us hope for the future. Memory is far from perfect, however. Our distorted or forgotten memories can also confuse and paralyze our functioning, especially in intimate relationships. The emotional stressors from early attachments, stored as nonconscious emotional memories, can give rise to phantom stress in adult intimacy. *When accurate memory fails, intimacy is a casualty.*

Stable, resilient and enduring connections integrate the elements of the *four guardians* in a unique balance. There is no fixed formula of just how much of each element or combination of the four guardians a couple needs. In my experience, relationships held hostage by phantom stressors rarely include all four of the guardians in the present.

How Phantom Stress Disconnected Lynn from Herself and Took Her Brain Hostage

The single most important result of phantom stress is that it breeds feelings of resentment and self-pity over time. These conscious emotions are rooted in the infantile attachment experiences of vulnerable dependency, anger, and fear of abandonment. They can also result from traumatic experiences later in life. Infant attachment research identifies three types of insecure attachment: ambivalent, avoidant, and disorganized. Stress research demonstrates that traumatic stress can permanently alter your sense of security in attachments and impair normal stress reactions. The emotions recreated by your phantom stress will reflect the feelings from your personal history in insecure attachments and traumatic stress. Phantom stress triggers inappropriate emotional responses and behavior based on the way your brain stores intense negative emotions.

In her Logosoma Brain Training, I helped Lynn reflect on the power of her phantom triggers. "If you could spot it when it occurs, phantom stress would appear as a kind of silly slip of emotion with no real harm done. But unfortunately, your brain gets the message through the same alarm system that tells you when real danger is near. Since phantom stress emerges from nonconscious brain maps drawn during past attachments, your brain thinks there's a real threat to its safety when triggered. It is literally hijacked by phantom stress. You spiral into self-doubt, acting out your fight/flight stress reaction with anger or fear. When phantom stress goes unchecked, it can create new negative memories of experiences that become long-lasting feelings of self-pity and resentment. You have become a hostage to the emotional script of a "victim" of all of your past experiences. Your dad's bankruptcy, his slow, alcoholic suicide, and your mother's resentment of his failures are all examples of traumatic and chronic stressors. These stressors have forced you to disconnect from your emotions and your body's sensations just to survive. Your husband's financial problems in the present caused you to replay your parents' tragedy of the past. You flee rather than stay and work it out together. You've become numb to your body's own needs and wishes. And along the way, you've lost your connection to the personal meaning that drove you to recover from your family's tragic experiences."

I continued explaining to Lynn, "When your brain gets stuck with feelings of resentment or self-pity as a result of repeated phantom stress, the stress becomes chronic. I call this a *hostage relationship*. You're not being held hostage by your mate, your boss, or your parents. Your brain is being held hostage by past stressors. So you must unravel the memories of emotion from the past with the trigger that activated your stress response in the present. Phantom stress locks your brain in patterns of disconnection and adversity that lead to chronic stress."

HOSTAGE RELATIONSHIPS

I often see individuals, couples, and families stuck in hostage relationships. They are distinguished by an inability to listen to themselves, to each other, or even to me. Their brains are imprisoned by feelings of oppression that are often self-inflicted or triggered by someone significant like a lover, a parent, a child, or a boss. I believe your brain can be taken hostage by *any relationship* that is emotionally charged and long term. When your brain's stress circuits are repeatedly triggered, you become trapped in a creeping emotional malignancy rooted in bad communication patterns, especially the ability to listen.

When your bids for attention often fail, crippling your ability to connect in open dialogue, your brain logs these as memories of emotional vulnerability. From minor disconnects to more emotionally charged disagreements, your ability to pay attention to the present situation spirals into permanent impairment. Your emotional assessment of your role in the relationship feels like a victim or a hostage. You begin to see others as the perpetrators of your misery.

Once the safe sanctuary of your attachment becomes contaminated with recurrent phantom stressors, feelings of distrust creep in. Your respect for the other is threatened. If left unchecked, the ability to think rationally and objectively becomes overwhelmed. You find yourself no longer able to communicate the simplest of things.

LYNN: "I CAN'T TAKE THIS STRESS ANY MORE!"

"My brain wasn't designed for the times we live in," Lynn complained. "Each day, I've got to get breakfast and review the newspaper, get myself ready, fight the traffic so I can make it to the office before nine. I don't sleep very well anymore. I wake up four or five times during the night. I used to have time to go to the gym three or for times a week, but now I'm just too exhausted. I don't even want to go. I know it would help me feel better but I've lost my motivation. I've gained ten pounds eating ice cream before bed every night for the last six months. I get so frazzled during the day sometimes, I start yelling at the receptionist for no reason. I know it doesn't help. It just keeps the stress levels up in the office. But at least it keeps me focused on my job. I used to love my job. It was a challenge. Now I feel burned out and I'm not even forty! And of course there's my mother's voice always nagging away in the back of my head whispering, 'When are you going to have a baby?' Dr. Romero, I just can't take the stress anymore!"

When it becomes nearly impossible to turn off the fight/flight/freeze mode of living and your own phantom stressors start creeping up at the office, you have got the formula for serious physical, emotional and professional problems.

ALLOSTATIC LOAD: YOUR BODY IS WEARING OUT

There is no getting away from it: when you combine daily stress with phantom stress, you are on your way to overloading your body's stress system, creating *allostatic load*. As your problems worsen, your physical, emotional, and relationship health are all compromised. Today, more than 50 percent of Americans identify stress as their number one health concern. And eight out of ten of our most commonly prescribed medications in the U.S. treat conditions related to stress—antidepressants, anti-anxiety medication, sleeping pills, gastric problems, and high blood pressure meds.

Marital stress research tells us that chronic stress produces a direct negative effect on the cardiovascular, endocrine, immune, and neurosensory mechanisms that undermine the health of both partners. Yale dermatologist Nicholas Perricone, MD, says that when you do not get enough sleep, the body produces excess cortisol, a hormone that breaks down skin cells. Getting enough rest produces more HGH (human growth hormone), which helps skin remain thick, more elastic, and less likely to wrinkle. It is no longer just a notion: stress *is* a silent killer. It suppresses then destroys our immune system; it is the prime mover in depression; and it destroys our resistance to other forms of attack from illness.

A recent Scandinavian study of a large group of healthy men demonstrated that, over time, their attitudes alone could have powerful positive or negative effect on their health. At the age of forty, the subjects were examined and found to be in good health. Then they were asked two simple questions:

Do you believe that you can affect the course of your life?

Do you believe that you will accomplish your life dreams?

The answer, either yes or no, divided them into two groups: the optimists who felt empowered to change their lives, and the pessimists who felt they were powerless. Five years later, they were reexamined and the degree of morbidity, measured by high blood pressure, heart disease, alcoholism, divorce, diabetes, and gastrointestinal disorders, was dramatically greater in the pessimistic group.

The interrelation between stress and the immune system is a two-way street. While stress can make you sick, positive beliefs can make you well. The complex connections between health and belief lie in the molecular changes in the brain that occur during learning. Learning actually alters the architecture of the synaptic connections in your nervous system. When accompanied by positive beliefs, these changes have shown to have positive effects in helping your immune system combat diseases, especially those caused by stress.

When your overstimulated stress system takes on an allostatic load attempting to adapt to modern life, your emotional connections can also be taken hostage. Your body will struggle to heal any kind of wound until a safe place has been recovered. A safe sanctuary is essential if you are to reconnect with yourself.

LYNN: LEARNING TO RECONNECT WITH HERSELF BY NEUTRALIZING NEGATIVE ASSESSMENTS

Lynn knew that she had to change her attitudes and behaviors, but she felt clueless about where to begin. Her feelings of helplessness and hopelessness were keeping her awake at night. In fact, all of the lifestyle habits that protect us from stress, a good night's sleep, exercise, a healthy diet, and secure emotional bonds, were all impaired. Lynn was accumulating a whopping allostatic load. It was causing her irritated bowel, weight gain, insomnia, and her irritability and hair-trigger temper with others. Putting it simply, Lynn was burning out.

"I'm ready to get help," Lynn said, finally beginning to surrender, "but I don't want to take medication if I don't have to." Lynn had always overcome her problems alone. By steeling herself against adversity and carrying on with a sense of self-determination, all of her problems seemed to be overcome or abandoned. Lynn's high standards kept her motivated. She was her own worst critic. But her extreme independent attitude was clearly not working. Lynn had hit rock bottom. But now, she was finally beginning to realize that "doing it my way" was a dead end. On the road to recovery, Lynn felt a deep sense of relief in surrendering her need to control everything in her life. Her go-it-alone style could finally be changed. She was beginning to accept the guidance she so desperately needed.

"I've become so sensitive that almost any comment about me feels like a negative assessment or criticism," Lynn confided. "Even simple observations about my appearance or my work performance can trigger a stress reaction. I get so defensive or snap back with some acid remark. I don't like what's happening to me."

One of the most common triggers for phantom stress is an explicit or implicit negative assessment. "One windy morning, I entered the office and my hair was tussled," Lynn recalled. The receptionist pointed it out, and I barked at her, "Who asked you! You're not my mother!"

Lynn's first lesson in Logosoma Brain Training was learning to identify when her body was triggered by stress. Lynn's primary phantom stressor was not the result of insecure attachment during her early childhood, but rather it emerged from the traumatic financial and emotional disaster her family suffered when she was a young teenager. Her shame trigger was organized around financial insecurity. Once she identified her stressful money conversation as the primary trigger for most of her chronic worries, she learned to refocus her attention on her present context.

"I feel like part of me is hiding behind a screen that I call financial security. When I was fourteen I became a shell-shocked teenager, numbed by my family's financial downfall."

Lynn eventually learned to accept her past as a tragedy rather than blame her parents for ruining her life. "I realize that my job now is to reconnect with this part of me. I need to give myself the emotional security I lost when I was fourteen," she reflected.

BRAIN SCAN: THE LONG SHADOW OF SHAME

Lynn came to see how every negative assessment she made of herself or heard in the course of a day hit the same trigger: the pain of shame and humiliation. "'Sticks and stones will break my bones, but names will never hurt me' is just not true," Lynn mused.

"When I'm struck by one of these negative emotional blows, my defensive shield goes up instantaneously. All I can do is flee or retaliate," Lynn realized.

The phantom stress linked to negative assessments often goes all the way back to the "terrible twos" when brain circuits for shame were molded by your mother teaching you right from wrong. By shaming you with negative assessments of your behavior ("Bad boy!" "Bad girl!" "Don't do that!"), parents use shunning as a method to socialize their children. Good boys and girls do it "mommy's way." You began hearing this before your brain could form retrievable memories. In other words, the foundation of your brain networks for shame is nonconscious memories waiting to be triggered by an embarrassing social situation. A thousand times as a child your brain was deeply ingrained with the neural architecture that you know as your conscience. When shaming has been overdone in childhood, the result is often a self-critical perfectionist with low self-esteem and high achievements. As a teenager, you began to test out more complex oppositional attitudes and behaviors by trying life your way as the beginning of becoming true to yourself. Many parents of teenagers find the resulting talking back stressful and fail fully to understand the developmental necessity of this behavior as an essential ingredient in a healthy identity.

Whether you are two, twelve, twenty, or fifty, a negative assessment initiates a startle response in your brain. It mobilizes your allostatic systems for an adaptive response. When a negative assessment, even a tiny one, comes unexpectedly from someone with whom you are connected, your brain is slightly stressed.

Lynn had a history of sensitivity to implicit criticism from her father. After his financial ruin, Lynn's father paid very little attention to his daughters. Lynn took this as an implicit disapproval of her, so she became a skilled people-pleaser, an excellent student aiming to win approval from her teachers.

MANAGING YOUR CONNECTIONS

Managing your connections means regulating—not controlling—your emotions. This skill is critical for preventing chronic stress. You begin by securing an attachment with your own body, your sense of personal meaning, and establishing healthy emotional bonds with others. (This will be discussed in detail in Part II.)

When I listen to the life stories of my patients, I help them assess how each of the four guardians of attachment is working in their connection with themselves and their relationships. How well can you regulate your emotions when you get triggered? How secure are you in your own body, in your sense of self? How much memory do you share with others? Do you feel like you have a sense of We in your relationships? Do you feel that you communicate your connectedness in language?

We are natural born storytellers, and we like telling stories about ourselves. Talking and sharing stories with others can enhance memories and amplify their emotional value. The more you think and talk about your experiences, the better you understand what happened in your past. Also, by sharing stories you improve your record of important events with others, your We memories. When you discuss and rehearse a We experience, you protect this memory, at least partially, from transience. Memories that you feel are not important enough to ponder or mention tend to fade more quickly. A resilient and enduring story of We is etched into your memory banks by sharing stories of your emotional experiences.

I also ask people about their emotional bonds. Are your bonds vibrant and thriving? Do you feel physically connected? Some tell me that they regularly make love with their partners but are emotionally distant and aloof. Others tell me that they are cuddly and warm but make love rarely. Having heard every variation on the four guardians of intimacy, my goal is to help each person understand what they need, what they want, how to make requests, how to make assessments, and most importantly, how to listen to themselves and to others. This is the practice required to manage your connections.

YOU AND THE WE STORY

You will not feel safe and be able to recover from the stresses of daily life until all four guardians are working within your relationships. This starts with your relationship to "me, myself, and I." Taking a personal inventory of the elements in your connections provides a map for managing the stress in your relationships.

There is no right or wrong formula for connectedness. There is no perfect score or percentage. But if you suppress your emotions and avoid personal issues, sooner or later trouble will surface. It is important to communicate your wishes and needs. We need to listen deeply to the wishes and needs of others. That is how you will create a We story for all of your relationships. Your formula will be unique, custom-designed, by and for you and your relationships. In chapter 3, the connectedness inventory invites you to complete a self-assessment exercise.

QUIET MOMENTS OF REFLECTION

Reflections on Stress

1. I accept that stresses from my everyday life and phantom stressors from my past can combine to overwhelm me.
2. When my body and brain are overwhelmed by stress, I can become irritable, irrational, and distrustful.
3. When my body and brain are overwhelmed by stress, I accept that I can feel like a hostage—vulnerable and devalued.
4. When my body and brain are overwhelmed by stress, I accept that I can act impulsively and destructively within my relationships.
5. I declare that I want to learn and practice ways to change these patterns of thinking, feeling, and behaving.

Reflections on Connectedness

1. I accept that successful connections spring from secure attachment, from the balanced coordination between two bodies and two life stories working together to create a shared narrative with a positive emotional charge, a We story.
2. The foundation of my relationships is made of physical contact, emotional bonds, the stories shared in language, and the memories I make with others: the four guardians of secure attachment.
3. I accept that connectedness is a reciprocal, dynamic, ever-changing process.
4. I declare that I want to create and nurture a positive emotional We story with my relationships.

Chapter 3

THE POWER OF WE:
THE CONNECTEDNESS INVENTORY

One word frees us of all the weight and pain of life: that word is love.

—**Sophocles**

Scientific research has proven time and time again that common sense is usually our most reliable guide. So, many of us will not be surprised to learn the best defenses against stress are quite simple: a good night's sleep, a regular exercise program, a healthy diet, and secure emotional bonds. By cultivating awareness of your body and owning up to who you really are, you can repair the insecure attachments from your past and form new connections in the present. Logosoma Brain Training will help you articulate the state and characteristics of your stress. Following my four-step program will empower you to develop and strengthen your optimal adaptive resilience, your defense against the ravages of chronic stress. More importantly, I will teach you how to recover from the terrible effects of stress-related damage so you can end your suffering, regain your resilience, and reconnect. By practicing the skills taught in Logosoma Brain Training, you are on the path to its ultimate goal: the cultivation of well-being through connectedness to yourself, to others and to the world around you. I call this the *power of We*.

Are You Stressed Out?

Are you stressed out? Do you sometimes feel disconnected from the people, places, and things that give your life meaning? Is life changing too fast for you?

I use two proprietary methods, the logosoma stress inventory and the connectedness inventory, to help my patients assess and plan a strategy for becoming more resilient to stress in the future.

We know that life changes are stressful. Successfully adapting to new challenges can take a toll on your physical and emotional health. Holmes and Rahe devised a way of measuring the impact of certain life changes on our health. The logosoma stress inventory, a specially customized version of the classic Holmes and Rahe stress scale, is designed to help you assess the stress in your body and life story.

How strong are your emotional connections? How secure are your connections to your body, your intimate relationships, your career, and your environment? The connectedness inventory will help you develop a map of your personal network of connectedness.

When your stress system is overloaded, your body begins to break down, bit by bit. The wear and tear of stress can disconnect you from the fabric of good health. Imbalance can occur in your stress hormones and immune system. Disruption can emerge in your personal eating habits, exercise, and sleep. Even the security in your relationships that support you at home, at work, and in your community can be damaged. The connectedness inventory assesses the state of just how connected you are. Much like a six-month dental check-up or a 3,000-5,000 mile oil change in your car, I developed the connectedness inventory to evaluate the strength of my patients' four guardians of secure attachment (skinship, emotional bonds, language, and memory). I have found that empowering individuals, couples, and families to develop routine maintenance of the four guardians helps ward off chronic stress and neutralize phantom stressors. The result is improved relationship satisfaction.

The level of satisfaction you experience in a relationship will play a critical role in defining what a healthy emotional bond is for you. Marital studies comparing high and low partnership fulfillment have demonstrated that couples with a high satisfaction rating are healthier and live longer; not surprisingly, unhappy couples suffer many more negative health consequences.

Logosoma Brain Training aims to strengthen your emotional ties with all of your life connections. In my experience with individuals, couples, and families, I have found the best way to help people improve their resilience to the stress of everyday life, and especially the insidious effects of phantom stress, is to teach them just what elements they need to make a healthy emotional bond.

Am I Stressed Out? The Logosoma Stress Inventory

The logosoma stress inventory is derived from the classic Holmes and Rahe self-assessment social readjustment scale. The items in the inventory have been rearranged in different categories according to what I call *developmental narrative domains*. The original weighting and scoring of each item has been kept true to the original Holmes and Rahe inventory. By completing the questionnaire, you will be able to assess your risk of illness caused by the physiologic overload of the stress system.

Logosoma Brain Training uses the Holmes and Rahe scale to evaluate four narrative domains of your life story: identity/embodiment, relationships, career, and environment.

To assess your own stress now, circle the statements below that apply to you, add them up, and compare your score with the table below.

IDENTITY / EMBODIMENT

63 detention in jail or other institution
53 major personal injury or illness
40 sex difficulties
28 outstanding personal achievement
24 revision of personal habits
19 change in recreational habits
17 major purchase, such as a new car
16 change in sleeping habits
15 change in eating habits
12 Christmas or holiday observance
11 minor violation of the law

RELATIONSHIPS

100	death of a spouse
73	divorce
65	marital separation
63	death of a close family member
50	marriage
45	marital reconciliation
44	change in health or behavior of family member
40	pregnancy
39	gain of new family member through birth, adoption, or marriage
37	death of close friend
35	change in number of arguments with partner
29	son or daughter leaves home
29	trouble with in-laws
26	partner begins or stops work
15	change in number of family gatherings

CAREER

47	fired from work
45	retirement
39	major business readjustment
38	change in financial state
36	change to a different line of work
31	taking on a new mortgage
30	foreclosure on a mortgage or loan
29	change in responsibilities
26	starting or finishing school
23	trouble with boss
20	change in working hours or conditions

ENVIRONMENT

25	change in living conditions
20	change in residence
20	change in schools
19	change in church activities
18	change in social activities
13	vacation

Holmes and Rahe estimate that 35 percent of us with a score less than 150 will experience a stress-related illness within two years. This increases to 51 percent for those of us between 150 and 300, and an alarming 80 percent for scores over 300.

SCORING FOR THE HOLMES-RAHE SOCIAL READJUSTMENT SCALE

Less than 150 life-change units	=	30% chance of developing a stress-related illness
150-299 life-change units	=	50% chance of illness
More than 300 life-change units	=	80% chance of illness

Although you might not be able to control the stressful events in your life, you can learn to change the way you respond to them. The negative effects of stress can be reduced by getting enough rest, exercise, a healthy diet, and taking time to do the things you want to do.

One of the most important defenses you have against stress lies in your emotional connectedness to others. Recent science shows that resilience to stress is optimized by developing strong, positive emotional connections. This is reflected in the larger number of items in the relationship category above and the high scores given to each of these elements.

How Well Connected Am I? The Connectedness Inventory

Your answers to the connectedness inventory (CI) questions reflect who you are by evaluating the connectedness you have to your body, your sense of self, and your relationships. I often use the CI to map the texture and durability of my patients' and their relationship networks, creating a written history of what I call their Logosoma (story/body) profiles.

Consider each statement, and then fill in the blank with one of the three choices (often, sometimes, rarely), for each of the four parts: physical, emotion, language, and memory. Do not spend too long on each question. Your first reaction will usually be the best and most accurate response, but if you want to change an answer, just cross it out and change it. Please answer every question. When you come to the end of the questions, you will be able to score it.

When filling out the CI, *you* are the reference point: *your* needs, *your* wishes, *your* point of view, *your* values, and *your* beliefs. The questions will help you to identify areas causing stress in your relationships. Your answers will help identify problems you may not be conscious of, those that trigger anger and frustration for no apparent reason. The CI will also help to make your existing problems much clearer. Either way, I invite you to use your answers as indicators of particular areas in your relationships that may be beneficial for you to reflect upon.

Please keep in mind that the simplicity of the CI helps focus your attention on categories critical to healthy, long-term, and resilient connections. It clearly does not assess all areas of your relationships. The CI does not replace clinical assessment or therapy. Your answers are meant to stimulate reflection, helping you to identify potential problems or ongoing stress.

Read every statement carefully and indicate which option applies best to you. You might run across questions describing situations that do not apply to you at all. In such cases, select an answer that would be most likely if you ever found yourself in such a situation.

CONNECTEDNESS INVENTORY

Answer all the questions before attempting to score the inventory.

Part I: Body Connections
(a) Physical Relationship: Skinship
Complete the sentence by choosing one:
1. Rarely   2. Sometimes   3. Often

1. I _____ like myself when I look in the mirror.
2. I _____ feel calmed by touching people I love.
3. I _____ love my body when I'm having sex with my partner.
4. I _____ feel gratitude about the state of my body.
5. I_____ feel relaxed after sexual activity with my partner.

Add each rating for subtotal (a): _____

(b) Physical Relationship: Skinship
Complete the sentence by choosing one:
1. Often   2. Sometimes   3. Rarely

6. I _____ avoid touching my family and friends.
7. I _____ avoid meeting new people.
8. I _____ feel unsure if should hug someone of the same sex.
9. I _____ have sweaty palms when I shake hands.
10. I _____ feel uncomfortable when my family or friends touch me.

Add each rating for subtotal (b): _____

Total skinship score (a + b): _____

(a) Emotional Bonds
Complete the sentence by choosing one:
1. Rarely   2. Sometimes   3. Often

1. I _____ feel safe when I am with someone I love.
2. I _____ feel warmth when my partner/ friend/ family looks at me.

3. I _____ feel good when anyone in my family listens to me.
4. I _____ relax when my friends compliment me.
5. I _____ can fall asleep cuddling with my partner.

Add each rating for subtotal (a): _____

(b) Emotional Bonds
Complete the sentence by choosing one:
1. Often   2. Sometimes   3. Rarely

6. I _____ feel lonely when I am with friends or family.
7. I _____ feel ignored in social settings
8. I _____ feel jealous when I see others flirting.
9. I _____ avoid discussing finances with my friend or family.
10. I _____ laugh with my friends and family.

Add each rating for Subtotal (b): _____

Total emotional bond score (a + b): _____

Part II: Life Story Connections
   (a) Language
   Complete the sentence by choosing one:
   1. Rarely   2. Sometimes   3. Often

1. My partner/family/friend is _____ a good listener when I speak.
2. My partner/family member/friend _____ asks me how I feel.
3. My partner/family member/friend _____ uses "we" in conversation.
4. My partner/family member/friend _____ shares his/her fears with me.
5. My partner/family member/friend _____ shares his/her dreams with me.

Add each rating for subtotal (a): _____

(b) Language
Complete the sentence by choosing one:
1. Often   2. Sometimes   3. Rarely

6. Other people _____ interrupt me when I am talking.
7. Other people _____ change conversations to "all about them."
8. I _____ rely on others' opinions above mine.
9. I _____ complain if my friend or family member answers his or her cell phone no matter what we are doing.
10. When I am upset with someone I _____ give the "silent treatment."

Add each rating for subtotal (b): _____

Total language score (a + b): _____

(a) Memories
Complete the sentence by choosing one:
1. Rarely   2. Sometimes   3. Often

1. My partner/family member/friend and I _____ remember things alike.
2. My partner/family member/friend and I _____ discuss our past.
3. My partner/family member/friend _____ creates special moments for me.
4. My partner/family member/friend and I _____ have special songs/music together.
5. My partner/family member/friend _____ remembers our anniversary.

Add each rating for subtotal (a): _____

(b) Memories
Complete the sentence by choosing one:
1. Often   2. Sometimes   3. Rarely

6. I _____ remember every mistake others make.
7. I _____ remind others of their negative characteristics.

8. I _____ remind others of our past fights.
9. I _____ forget to do favors for others when I am asked.
10. I _____ forget family events.

Add each rating for subtotal (b): _____

Total memory score (a + b): _____

SCORING YOUR CI

Each statement scores one, two, or three points. "Rarely" scores one point, "Sometimes" scores two points, and "Often" scores three points. The top score in each category is 30 points—a rating of three points × 10 questions. The minimum score in each section is 10 points—a rating of one point × 10 questions. Each section should be scored separately. At the end, you will have four total scores, one score for each section.

RATING YOUR CI SCORES

The CI score measures patterns of attachment on a high-low frequency scale, using the categories of the four guardians—skinship (physical contact), emotional bonding, language, and memory. Remember, there is no right score, no perfect balance. What is reflected here is the profile and texture of your attachments.

Low frequency (L)   10-16
Middle frequency (M)   17-24
High frequency (H)   25-30

You can now add the rating of L, M, or H next to the raw score.

Skinship: _____
Emotional Bonding: _____
Language: _____
Memory: _____

INTERPRETING YOUR CI SCORES: A PERSONAL VALUE

Interpreting your CI profile is a very personal matter. You are not a just a number! This is not a statistical inventory that compares your score against others. The interpretation of the CI is subjective. As I tell my private patients, "Only you can weigh the importance of these scores."

For example, Mary Lou and Tommy both scored high frequency in memory and emotional bonding, middle frequency in language, and low frequency in skinship. Although most of us would not be satisfied by such a low skinship score, it was more than enough to keep the couple content. Happy with the way things were, they did not want change the fabric of their partnership.

For each of the four categories, ask yourself the following questions.

1. How important is this category for me?

If you feel that the importance of a category is high for you and your score is low, you will clearly want to focus on making changes here. For example, if your skinship score is low, you may want to explore your personal history of physical intimacy to track down patterns of dissatisfaction or avoidance in your childhood. With the Logosoma Brain Training in Part II of this book, you will learn to create a meaningful script for action, helping you change your patterns and strengthen your physical bonds. The goal is wellbeing, not some idealized behavior.

2. Am I hurting or unsatisfied in this category?

Reflecting on your body, your emotions, your memories, and your current life story will facilitate a connection with your own personal truth, the core meaning of your life story. Dissatisfaction in any attachment is a direct result of the loss of focused attention (listening or respect) and/or commitments to action (promises). Tending to disappointments is a top priority for mending your bonds with others.

3. Do I want to change my score?

Motivation for change springs from dissatisfaction with the status quo. By being honest about who you are, you can spark the motivation to transform yourself into the person you want to be. Part II will give you the tools.

4. Do I feel that I am the problem in my relationships?

An optimistic attitude actually enhances your brain's ability to change stuck patterns of emotion, thinking, and behavior. To optimally learn new habits you will find it immensely helpful to cultivate an attitude of openness to look at your self-sabotaging behaviors. Taking your own inventory will clear the way to develop new patterns of interaction for healthier, more resilient connections.

5. Am I willing to change my attitudes and behaviors to affect my score?

Willingness to change is the key to creating motivation for the Logosoma practice. Identifying the obstacles in the way of your personal satisfaction will help liberate you from the negative patterns and attitudes developed from insecure attachments in your past. By learning new behaviors, you will create the clearing to reconnect, securely this time, to yourself and to others in the present.

6. How will changing myself in any category help me?

Your assessment of the value of any of these four categories will determine what kind of changes you will make. Remember, the point of all this is to recover the story of We by overcoming stress and reactivating the calm and connect circuits in your brain.

7. Can I talk with my partner/family/friends about my concerns in this category?

Discussing charged issues in any of these categories may require the expression of negative assessments. Before you negatively assess anyone, ask if he or she is ready to hear criticism that may be painful. This will help both of you prepare for a tough talk about what is not satisfying in your relationship.

Give your answers some thought. This is just the beginning of strengthening your connectedness to yourself and to others. Any lasting changes you make will affect those who are emotionally connected to you. The CI maps the territory in your relationships that you will want to explore and redesign.

Now that you have assessed your connectedness network, you are ready to move on to Part II: Logosoma Brain Training.

PART II

"The human mind is so powerful, the connections between perception and physiological response is so strong, that we can set off the fight or flight response by just imagining ourselves in a threatening situation."

Bruce McEwen

Chapter 4

INTRODUCTION TO LOGOSOMA BRAIN TRAINING

Don't compromise yourself. You're all you've got.
—**Janis Joplin**

I invite you to embark on Logosoma Brain Training, a four-step program that will change your brain to enable *healthy, resilient, authentic connections with yourself, your body, your partner, your family, your career, your community, and your environment.*

Logosoma Brain Training integrates principles from modern neuroscience, psychotherapy, and the ancient practice of meditation. The training program invites you to face your fears and be honest with yourself. I will teach you how to train your attention and refocus, a major factor in managing your impulsive, emotional reactions to stress. By liberating yourself from the bonds of phantom stressors, you will be able to refocus your attention on creating healthy emotional bonds, the foundation of connectedness.

Resilience to the everyday stress and to the triggers of your phantom stress starts with the integration of your brain circuitry for language and emotion—the memories of your life story—with the emotional connections to your body. The result of this life story/body integration is to form an authentic identity, a true self, your own genuine story of *me*. This is the optimal adaptive resilience to stress. Emerging honestly as who you really are puts you in the ideal position to create lasting connections.

I cannot say this strongly enough: making a commitment to change the patterns of connectedness starts with you—not with you *and* your partner or your family. By changing your attitudes and behaviors, by starting to be honest with yourself, you will gradually begin to rewire your brain circuits for optimal adaptive resilience. Of course, those around you may become confused by your new behavior at first. But do not worry! Hopefully, they will change along with you. Or at the very least, join you in a new dialogue.

The Logosoma Brain Training in this book uses the same coaching techniques that I use in my office. First, I listen to your story. Next, I help you to begin reflecting on the fears and wishes that have shaped your life story. When I work with couples and families, we begin by rediscovering the nuances of their life stories and what triggers their nonconscious body memories. Eventually, I train the couple or family to embrace a new sense of meaningful connectedness, to become "Team We."

TRAINING YOUR EFFORTFUL ATTENTION: MINDFUL AWARENESS

Logosoma Brain Training focuses on three goals for attentional training. First is just to relax, to recover from the daily stress triggers. This can be accomplished by a simple, repetitive focus on breathing or counting, also called "the relaxation response." Second is to focus on two questions to distinguish your false self from your true self: What am I afraid of? What are my wishes? Third is to cultivate a sense of deeper personal meaning by focusing on benevolent concepts like compassion, forgiveness, acceptance, gratitude, connectedness, and impermanence.

Mindful awareness is not a "mystical" exercise. You do not have to sit in a lotus position, *but you might want to consider using a scented candle to enhance your memory and relaxation*. Mindful awareness is an introspective and repetitive practice. Mindful awareness focuses your conscious attention inward, toward the flow of your own mental and emotional processes. By learning to observe your own thoughts like an independent spectator, you will begin to gain a sharpened awareness of exactly what you are thinking and feeling. Mindful awareness is critical to Logosoma Brain Training, to the building of new attitudes, habits, and language that will retrain your brain and reshape your connections with others.

The logosoma practice of mindful awareness is based on ancient meditation techniques from the Far East and the exciting new discovery of neuroplasticity, the brain's built-in ability to rewire itself and form new neuronal connections. In recent years, neuroscientists have proven your brain is not fixed but can actually be remodeled. Through focused attention over time, you can rewire your brain's synaptic connections. Neuroplasticity makes it possible for you to break old destructive habits by rewiring your brain to develop a new resilient sense of authenticity in your identity, longer lasting love with your mate, and emotionally secure bonds with your family and social network. This is exactly how emotional healing in psychotherapy works. By retelling your story, remembering old wounds, reflecting on patterns of self-sabotaging behaviors, and initiating new life patterns based on your wishes, you begin to rewire your brain to become your true self.

If you have never undertaken any meditation training, I recommend several books in the references. Getting started is easy. You can begin by simply sitting in a comfortable chair with your back straight and body relaxed. Your eyes should be slightly closed, focusing around six feet ahead on the floor. Try to focus on your breathing. This will be difficult at first. Thoughts and feelings will arise. But do not engage with them, just observe them and gently return to focusing on your breath. By practicing for fifteen minutes per day, in just a few weeks your attentional network will strengthen. Over time, mindful awareness will be one of the most important tools for helping you rewire your brain and reduce your vulnerability to stress triggers.

BRAIN SCAN: PRACTICE WITH PASSION

Our brain is a plastic organ. Far from being fixed, it is malleable, resilient, and responsive. The brain is constantly changing. Each experience not only modifies the way the brain works but also remodels and reconfigures its very structure. This process of modification is how we learn and remember. Neuroplasticity, the brain's ability to rewire itself through effortful focused attention, happens much more easily when preceded by strong emotions. Conscious awareness and reflection on strong emotional responses can promote the formation of new circuits for healthier patterns of behavior. Over time, repetition of these newly learned patterns can make the new circuitry permanent. As Donald Hebb, the father of neuroplasticity theory, explains: "Cells that fire together wire together." In practical terms, if you want a new habit to last, it is important to practice. The new circuits must be used or they atrophy and die. So remember—use it or lose it!

But mere practice is not quite enough. Let us suppose you are a violinist in an orchestra. The conductor has ordered you to improve your left-hand fingering of a particular piece. Rigorous repetitive movement of your fingers across the violin strings will increase the size of your brain map of the motor cortex dedicated to remembering fingering positions.

Imagine, however, that you are so not enthusiastic about playing the piece. You practice it, but half-heartedly. Unfortunately, no matter how many times you repeat the exercises, you will only experience a mild increase in remembering the left-hand fingering. But if you are passionate about expanding your skills, if you want to win the conductor's praise, you will bring an emotional charge to your practice that will allow for much greater neuroplasticity. When such adrenaline kicks in, it is much easier for the brain to create stronger, longer-lasting memory maps.

THE PROGRAM

The four steps of Logosoma Brain Training—what I call the four Rs—are the tools to help you rewire your brain, so your brain cells fire together in new, healthier patterns. By becoming ruthlessly honest and compassionate with yourself, by showing yourself authentically to your partner, and by respecting your boundaries in your family and social network, you begin the process of repairing and strengthening all of your emotionally charged social connections.

The four-step training will gradually become second nature to:

1. **Refuse** the stress invitation from others as well as from yourself
2. **Refocus** your attention to recover from stress triggers and retain your rational mental functions
3. **Reflect** to cultivate mindful awareness, the path to your authentic identity
4. **Reconnect** with others and recover the power of We

How long will it take until you to experience the changes that Logosoma Brain Training promises? Changes will come in accordance with the level of effort you make to refocus your attention and choose a new pattern of behavior. For instance, you can choose honesty instead of avoidance. In order to make these changes last, practice is required. When you practice with passion, the changes will come faster and last longer.

During your logosoma attentional training, you will be continually asked to comply with two requests: *listen* and *act*. You will focus your attention on listening to yourself and to others. You will act by following up the discovery of your personal truths, gleaned from self-investigation, with positive action. *Listening* and *acting* are the bookends of Logosoma Brain Training.

As you move through the four steps, you will find that each step blends into the next.

In step 1, you will learn to *refuse* invitations to stress conversations that trigger worry. You will use the tool of effortful attention to identify the triggers that cause a stress response in your body.

Step 2, will teach you how to *refocus* your attention away from the perceived threat that triggers adrenaline causing your body to freeze, fight or flee. Instead, I will show you how to refocus your attention toward healthy actions so you can begin to down-regulate your stress system and chill out. Refocusing away from the stress trigger allows you to recover your clear cognitive brain function.

Step 3 trains you to reflect, to shift your attention inward, and to distinguish your fears and false self from your wishes and your true self. When you find the core of your true self, you are ready to accept, validate, and love the person you really are. This gives you the freedom to show up in all of your relationships authentically, courageously, and respectfully.

The goal of the final step is to *reconnect* with others. A sanctuary of connectedness and strong emotional bonds with family and friends is the result of joint attention with others. In turn-taking communication, you create a shared narrative with those around you. The power of We will build a stress-resistant sanctuary to protect your most intimate relationships. You can show up as a true self and accept others as they are, making it possible to explore and express intense negative emotions in a safer context of trust and respect. Working conflicts through to resolution creates positively charged emotional memories. With these memories, you build a shared narrative experience and cultivate life-long bonds. These resilient connections form the foundation for the power of We.

Practicing the four Rs of Logosoma Brain Training will help you neutralize the charge of phantom stress triggers and reverse the ravages of chronic stress. With the new attitudes and behaviors learned in the training, you will begin to build an authentic sanctuary of We. You can begin to enjoy serious fun. And best of all, you can create and strengthen a new, profound connectedness with the world around you.

Congratulations—and let me welcome you to the Logosoma Brain Training. You are now ready to proceed to my four-step practice, the path toward finding your true self and enduring connectedness.

Logosoma Brain Training
Rewiring Your Brain's Stress Response

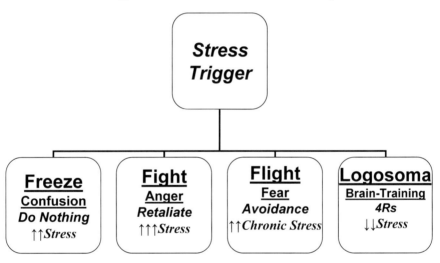

Stress Trigger

Freeze
Confusion
Do Nothing
↑↑Stress

Fight
Anger
Retaliate
↑↑↑Stress

Flight
Fear
Avoidance
↑↑Chronic Stress

Logosoma
Brain-Training
4Rs
↓↓Stress

STEP 1: REFUSE

Refuse the *Stress* Trigger

Pay Attention to your body's physical reaction to stress

Feel: ↑heart rate, ↑respiration, tight muscles, upset stomach

Accept that: "I've been triggered"
Do Not Act on Fear, Anger or Confusion

STEP 2: REFOCUS

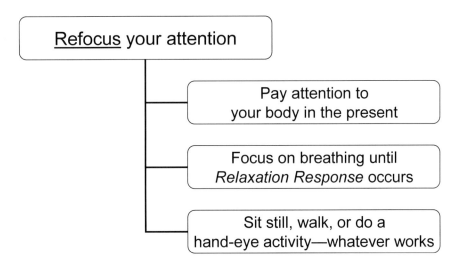

Refocus your attention

- Pay attention to your body in the present
- Focus on breathing until *Relaxation Response* occurs
- Sit still, walk, or do a hand-eye activity—whatever works

STEP 3: REFLECT

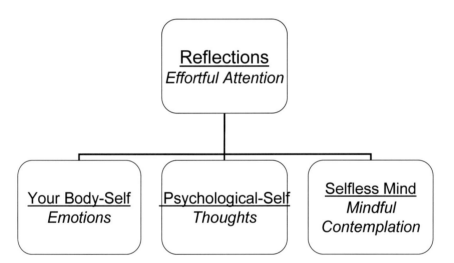

STEP 3-A: Your Body-Self

After calming your body, turn your attention inward to your _Emotions_

Reflect on your _Fear_
"What am I afraid of?"

Reflect on your _Confusion_
"What triggered my stress reaction?"

Reflect on your _Anger_
" What am I angry about?"

STEP 3-B: Your Psychological Self

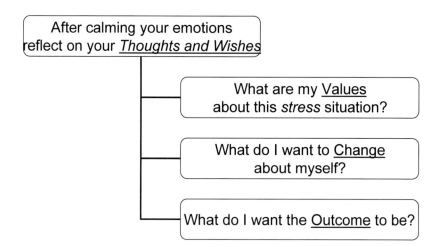

After calming your emotions reflect on your *Thoughts and Wishes*

What are my <u>Values</u> about this *stress* situation?

What do I want to <u>Change</u> about myself?

What do I want the <u>Outcome</u> to be?

STEP3-C: Your Psychological Self

Phantom Stress
Reflections on the _Past_

Phantom Stress trigger
"What does this stress remind me of?"

Recall _past stress memory_ in as
much detail as possible

Compare the _past stress_ event
with the _present stress_

STEP3-D: Your Psychological Self

Phantom Stress
Reflections on the _Present_

Meditate on "accepting"
the _past stress_ is _not-here-and-now_

Embrace the fact that
"I am NOT a helpless victim NOW!"

Embrace "gratitude" that
"I can change my reaction to stress."

STEP 3-E: Selfless Mind

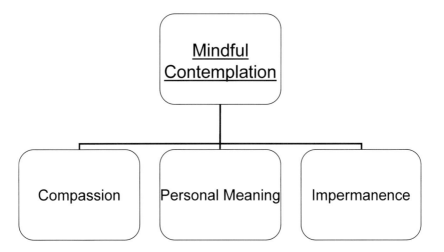

STEP 3-F: Selfless Mind

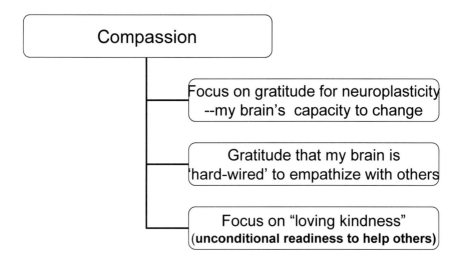

Compassion

Focus on gratitude for neuroplasticity
--my brain's capacity to change

Gratitude that my brain is
'hard-wired' to empathize with others

Focus on "loving kindness"
(unconditional readiness to help others)

STEP 3-G: Selfless Mind

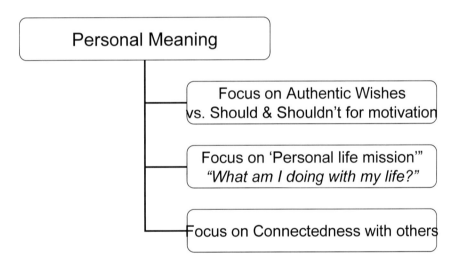

Personal Meaning

Focus on Authentic Wishes
vs. Should & Shouldn't for motivation

Focus on 'Personal life mission'"
"What am I doing with my life?"

Focus on Connectedness with others

STEP 3-H: Selfless Mind

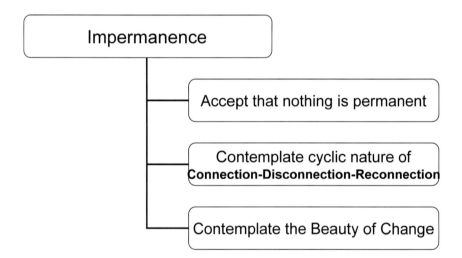

Impermanence

- Accept that nothing is permanent
- Contemplate cyclic nature of **Connection-Disconnection-Reconnection**
- Contemplate the Beauty of Change

STEP 4: RECONNECT

Stress Trigger→
Relationship
Disconnection

Freeze-Fight-Flight
↑↑↑ *Chronic Stress*

Reconnection
Conversation
↓↓↓ *Stress*

STEP 4-A: Reconnection Conversation

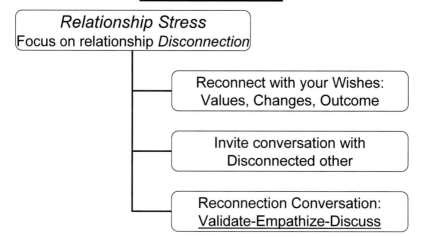

Relationship Stress
Focus on relationship *Disconnection*

Reconnect with your Wishes:
Values, Changes, Outcome

Invite conversation with
Disconnected other

Reconnection Conversation:
Validate-Empathize-Discuss

STEP 4-B: Reconnection Conversation

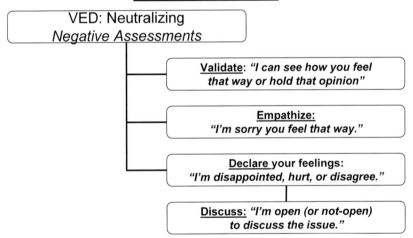

VED: Neutralizing *Negative Assessments*

Validate: *"I can see how you feel that way or hold that opinion"*

Empathize: *"I'm sorry you feel that way."*

Declare your feelings: *"I'm disappointed, hurt, or disagree."*

Discuss: *"I'm open (or not-open) to discuss the issue."*

STEP 4-C: Reconnection Conversation

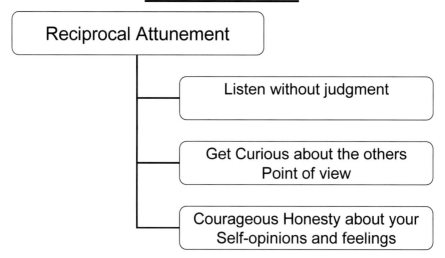

Reciprocal Attunement

Listen without judgment

Get Curious about the others Point of view

Courageous Honesty about your Self-opinions and feelings

STEP 4-D: Reconnection Conversation

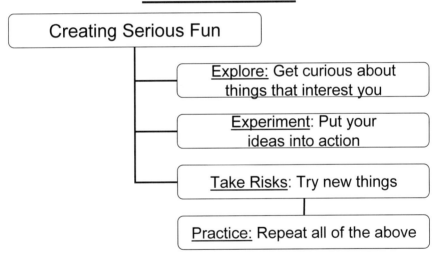

Creating Serious Fun

Explore: Get curious about things that interest you

Experiment: Put your ideas into action

Take Risks: Try new things

Practice: Repeat all of the above

STEP 4-E: Reconnection Conversation

Creating Positive Memories

Revisit positive experiences in conversation with others

Remember positive experiences alone and with others

Archive positive experiences with photos, journals, memorabilia

Chapter 5

STEP 1: REFUSE THE STRESS CONVERSATION

For one human being to love another; that is perhaps the most difficult of all our tasks, the ultimate, the last test and proof, the work for which all other work is but preparation.
— **Rainer Maria Rilke**

THE STRESS CONVERSATION

Conversations can be stressful. When a conversation is perceived as a threat to your well being, whether it is taking place internally or with another person, it can activate your allostatic response system. I call this a *stress conversation*. Typically triggered by the perception of a negative assessment, a stress conversation can cause a barrage of retaliatory thoughts which lead to self-sabotaging behaviors. Stress conversations are the number one cause of the destruction of the bond of trust and respect integral to any of your valued relationships.

Stress conversations trigger a *startle response* in your body. If left in the "on" position, your startle response can take your brain hostage by causing deadly chronic stress. As we have seen, chronic stress can distort your sense of self and destroy your physical health, your emotional bonds, and your ability to adapt successfully to your environment.

Unfortunately, nature has not wired your brain for the barrage of negative assessments you encounter every day in modern life. You are not wired to be resilient to the criticisms leveled at you by advertisers trying to humiliate you into buying their products or to deal with your cranky boss who never has a good word to say. And when you return home from work, the situation may be no better. Your allostatic system may be triggered even more by your critical partner or nagging children. In Logosoma Brain Training, one of the first questions I ask my patients is, "What conversations are you in?" and "What are they doing to your relationships?"

Brain Drama I: Sharon's Dilemma—"What's For Dinner?"

Sharon sat in my office and recalled an evening she had returned home from teaching a long, trying session of a children's dance class. All she could think about was having a peaceful evening and a cozy hug from her husband, Kevin.

"I was actually thinking we'd order in when I walked through the door. But when I jokingly said, 'What's for dinner?' Kevin looked at me like I'd just ordered him to scrub a toilet.

"'And just what makes you think *I'm* expected to plan dinner?' he said sarcastically. 'I've been working all day! I'm not your mother!'

"I saw his smile and knew he was just kidding. But Kevin's response shocked me. I felt an uncontrollable wave of heat in my body and a sick feeling in my stomach. I became confused; half of me wanted to run out the door or into the bedroom to cry. The other half felt like screaming and throwing something at him," Sharon recalled. "I was so startled that I bit my tongue. I couldn't speak anymore, so I just bottled up my emotions. I went cold and silent, leaving the room like I've done so often," she lamented.

Sharon felt anguish in her body, an unsettling, disturbing feeling that promotes the desire to flee, to fight, or to freeze. Was she actually in danger? No! But her brain and body were mobilizing as if Sharon were a facing a serious, life-threatening crisis. What Sharon experienced will happen to anyone in a long-term relationship. It can happen anytime or anywhere, at home, at work, or on vacation in a foreign country. A phantom stressor activated by a negative assessment can trigger your body and brain to prepare for a life or death struggle. So let us look at the cause such an inappropriate response.

BRAIN SCAN: WILD LIONS AND RUBBER SNAKES

Nature spent millions of years designing your survival circuitry. If you happened to see a lion running loose in your neighborhood, your first reaction would be to run like hell.

When your allostatic system has been activated, your body registers it first. Your hands become clammy and your neck muscles tighten. Neuroscientists call this a *bottom-up* message from the body to the brain. The brain receives the basic sensory information such as shape and color through the sensory thalamus, a limbic brain structure that acts like a switchboard for relaying incoming information from your five senses (sight, sound, smell, taste, and touch). It is also sent directly to your brain's fear center, the amygdala. When your amygdala receives information about something perceived as remotely unsafe or insecure, your autonomic nervous system and stress hormones kick in, mobilizing your body to perform incredible feats. We have all heard stories like the one about the old lady, who could barely walk, climbing a twenty-foot high tree to save her cat.

The superhuman strength triggered by the fight/flight response comes at a cost, however. It will dramatically impair your ability to think clearly and exercise good judgment. So you may out run the lion let loose in your neighborhood, only to run out into oncoming traffic and be hit by a car.

If, however, you were to see the lion in a safe environment, for example, in a cage at the zoo, your brain function actually becomes enhanced. Your ability to focus your attention is sharpened, your curiosity is stimulated, and your mood is improved. It would be natural for you to want to get close, to admire the lion's coat, to look at the size of his teeth, or to gaze into his eyes.

Now imagine that you are walking in the woods. You catch a glimpse of something black and coiled near your foot. Before you can think, you jump back, terrified that you are going to step on a snake. When the amygdala associates the coiled black object with its memory of a snake, it sends a startle message directly to the body through the autonomic nervous system and the limbic-hypothalamic-pituitary-adrenal axis (LHPA). This process is fast, measured in microseconds. And it is totally automatic and outside of consciousness. Neuroscientists call this the *low road*. Since this neural pathway is so short and swift, the information the amygdala receives is incomplete, not a clear representation of the trigger. In other words, you jump before you think, just as when you saw the lion in your neighborhood that caused you to run blindly into oncoming traffic.

While the bottom-up circuits send powerful survival signals of sensation and emotion from the body to the amygdala, the sensory thalamus also sends messages to the sensory cortex for *conscious reflection*. The cortex can look more closely at the information and compare it to conscious memories of past experience. After reflection, the cortex makes a decision about the safety of the situation and can send messages back to the body to direct the action. Now reconnected with the present situation, the cortex can get on with managing behavior. This pathway to the amygdala takes a little longer because it makes one more stop: the trigger travels from the thalamus to the cortex and then to the amygdala. It has been called the *high road* because the trigger makes that extra stop at the cortex where the information can be compared to actual memories of snakes: *"Is it moving? Does it taper at the end? Does it have a head? Does it look like the poisonous snakes I saw in the trail guidebook?"* This route takes longer to reach than the one to the amygdala, but when it gets there it is a much clearer representation of how threatening the trigger actually is.

When a negative assessment triggers a personal phantom stressor, loaded nonconsciously and repressed in your brain's memory bank, it can trigger a knee-jerk response, quickly shutting down your capacity for rational thought. The fight, freeze, or flight reaction sets you emotionally off balance. It is a shortcut to a meltdown, an argument or an emotional freeze-out. When you combine your phantom stressors from the past with the stress of everyday life, it is a prelude to overload. Neuroscientists call it *allostatic load*. We call it *stressed out*.

So how is knowing about the high and low road going to help you and your relationships? The good news is that you can train your cortex to send new messages to your body. These so-called top-down circuits from the brain to the body offer the possibility of developing new ways to manage the triggers from today's stress and yesterday's phantom stressors. By taking the high road, you can change your stress responses from knee-jerk, bottom-up, fight, or flight impulsivity to a pause-and-reflect, top-down response that is more thoughtful. Rather than react inappropriately to your partner's perceived negative assessment, you can stay cool and have a constructive conversation.

Nonetheless, whatever road you take, when you see something that looks like a snake, you are still going to jump. But through practice, you will be able to stop the stress response momentum and think, *"Oh, look at that! It's not moving. It's just an old piece of tire! I don't have to run. I don't have to attack. I don't have to freeze on the spot. I can continue on through the woods and enjoy the rest of my walk!"*

Just as you can mistake a piece of a tire for a snake, you can also mistake your partner or boss for a critical parent. Phantom stressors triggered by negative assessments are one of the main causes of what I call a *hostage relationship*. It occurs when two bodies, two life stories, and two brains become cohostages locked in patterns of disconnect and adversity as a result of chronically elevated stress. To be clear, it is your partnership itself that is being held hostage, not either one of you by the other. Misperceiving someone as a critical parent can trigger your survival physiology, causing you to act out a fight/flight scenario. The problem is, most people do not go back and take a look at what actually threatened them. They have not learned to use their reflective skills to process their stress responses.

SHARON'S STRUGGLE WITH THE NUMBER ONE PHANTOM STRESS TRIGGER: NEGATIVE ASSESSMENTS

So let us return to Sharon and Kevin's "What's for dinner?" conversation. How did it turn adversarial? Kevin perceived Sharon's innocent query more as a command than a question, causing him to overreact. In my sessions with Sharon, we discovered the roots of her sensitivity to criticism. Sharon grew up with a critical, perfectionist mother. Ever since she was a little girl, she was forced to submit to her mother's unreasonable commands and shaming. A trained dancer, Sharon sublimated her mother's perfectionism by pushing her body to extremes in order to master dance moves. She was her own taskmaster. When Kevin made a snide comment, she felt that he made a negative assessment of her very being, much like her mother did when she was a child. Sharon's response to Kevin's comments was a rapid mobilization of her survival physiology. She felt as if she were still a little girl struggling to survive another round of shaming and punishment from her critical mother.

Brain Scan: Coaching Your Amygdala

Every time a negative assessment slips from your lips, you implicitly send your partner back to the shame training of childhood when a mother or father bellowed out: "Do not write on the walls with crayons! Don't jump on your bed! Stop hitting you sister!" This is how your amygdala learned shame—from big mommy or big daddy's brain to your little amygdala. No matter how calm you may have been just before you heard it, each time a negative assessment is verbalized against you, it will trigger a nonconscious shame response in your body. The shame response can trigger a phantom stressor from your past. A phantom stressor can become activated by something as simple as a disapproving expression on your partner's face, by a clipped response, a snub, or a criticism. Overt negative expressions like being yelled at, manipulated, disrespected, or ignored are much more potent in conjuring the phantom stress invader from the depths of your brain.

Step 1 of Logosoma Brain Training, *refuse the stress invitation*, is focused on increasing awareness of your amygdala. You will learn to identify when your amygdala has been triggered by looking for the first signs of your body's stress reaction. Listening to your body and identifying the tell-tale signs of being triggered is a practice. Each time you experience a startle response, you will be able to identify that your amygdala has been triggered and your stress hormones are flowing. Your body may be telling you to freeze, fight, or flee, but Logosoma Brain Training will help you choose a new response to this physiological trigger. By learning how to rein in the amygdala's hair-trigger, to say no to the invitation to a stress conversation, you open the way for a very different outcome to phantom stress.

How to Refuse the Invitation to a Stress Conversation

You can now begin to see how your brain's survival circuits can cause trouble in your relationships. Once your amygdala is triggered, you can become a hostage to your own stress hormones, triggered by an endless cycle of swapping negative assessments with your partner. So, one way to begin neutralizing phantom stress is to refuse the invitation into toxic stress conversations. By saying "no" to stress conversations, you will begin to recover the sanctuary you call home.

So, let us begin to put your Logosoma Brain Training in gear.

LOGOSOMA SKILL: "I'VE BEEN TRIGGERED!"

We have established how the amygdala can be triggered by an event in the present or as association from the past. But now when it happens, I want you to start saying, "I've been triggered." You can say this out loud or to yourself, depending on the situation. This is the first step to declining invitations to stress conversations. With practice, you will be able to start really focusing attention on your body. This skill will enable you to start identifying the subtle hints your body gives you when it has been triggered.

The next time you notice tightness in your stomach, I want you to imagine you are playing a competitive sport and the referee has just thrown down a red flag indicating a foul play. You can referee your own stress response by announcing: "I've been triggered." You may want to develop a personalized cue when it involves other people. The cue can be a phrase or a word that acts as a stress alert, like "Time out." Using this declaration will mark a symbolic change in your perception of how stress reactions emerge. You will begin to take personal responsibility for your body state, naming stress as the enemy, not someone else.

Let us listen again to Kevin and Sharon in their "What's for dinner?" stress conversation. But this time, let us explore some new responses to their old stress patterns. By following the Logosoma Brain Training step of refusing the trigger, Sharon and Kevin will learn how to navigate their phantom stress triggers. So can you!

BRAIN DRAMA II: STRESS CONVERSATION BEFORE AND AFTER

Here is the script before Logosoma Brain Training:

Sharon: "What's for dinner?"
Kevin: "And just what makes you think *I'm* expected to plan dinner? I've been working all day! I'm not your mother!"
Sharon: "You don't have to be nasty about it."
Kevin: "I'm sick to death of being responsible for everything. I work too! Or haven't you noticed?"

Sharon: "Look, I'm exhausted. I thought you could order dinner for both of us."

Kevin: "You thought wrong! I'm not your maid or your mother! I'm your hard-working husband. And I'm just as exhausted as you!"

Sharon goes silent and withdraws into the bedroom.

Now let us look at the same situation after Logosoma Brain Training using the new "I've been triggered" technique of refusing the stress conversation:

Sharon: "What's for dinner?"

Kevin: "And just what makes you think *I'm* expected to plan dinner? I've been working all day! I'm not your mother!"

Although Sharon's stress response system is just about ready to blow, she starts paying attention to the symptoms in her body, to the knots forming in her stomach. Her awareness makes it possible to throw down the red flag for dealing with her stress. Rather than engage, Sharon's going to decline the stress conversation this time.

Sharon says: "I'm sorry Kevin, but I've been triggered. I really want to avoid a fight and another terrible evening. So I need some time to cool down. Please give me fifteen minutes. I'll try to calm down and talk with you then."

KEVIN'S POSSIBLE RESPONSES: THE HOSTAGE

1. "What do you mean? What did I do this time? Why am I always the bad guy?"

This is the typical response of someone caught in the story of a hostage victim. Although Kevin seems to take the blame, he's actually making an implicit negative assessment of Sharon. What he is really saying is that Sharon is being unfairly critical of him, rather than the other way around.

LOGOSOMA SKILL: THE VED SCRIPT FOR PROTECTION FROM NEGATIVE ASSESSMENTS

Sharon's best response is to deflect Kevin's passive-aggressive guilt trip. Instead she uses the Logosoma VED script, my three-part solution for protection from negative assessments: validate, empathize then discuss. In this particular stress conversation, it would work like this:

Validate: "I can see how you feel criticized by what I said."
Empathize: "I'm sorry you feel this way about it."
Discuss: "If you'd like, after I cool down, we can have a conversation about what just happened."

If Kevin insists on an immediate answer, Sharon must be firm and repeat the message: "I've been triggered and I need 15 minutes to cool down."

2. "That's well and good, but I'd like to know now!"

Be firm and follow the prescription above. Repeat your message and take your fifteen minutes.

3. "Good. Take your time. I'd rather talk to you when you're not so keyed up."

This is an excellent response from a caring and respectful husband. It underscores how joint attention facilitates a calming and connecting experience.

Q&A—QUESTIONS FROM MY PATIENTS

Q: **My husband can't take anything that sounds like criticism. When I say, "I've been triggered," he doesn't leave me alone, he just gets even angrier. What do I do?**

A: Your first act should be to refuse to participate in the escalating hostage relationship situation the two of you have created. Both of you are too full of stress hormones to think clearly. If your partner is stressed out and still persists in carrying on a stressful argument, the best thing that you can do is decline, decline, decline.

The wisest course of action is to remove yourself from the situation. If refusing the stress conversation seems impossible to do in the long term, you may even have to physically remove yourself from your home. Before leaving, make sure to declare, "I'll be back." You might stay with a parent, sibling, or friend for an hour or a day to give your partner a chance to cool down. Once you have left, call back to reassure your partner that you want a follow-up conversation.

While this option may sound drastic, taking yourself out of your home will show your partner that you are truly committed to self-respecting action. You want him to know you are serious about making changes, starting with your own behavior. Temporarily leaving will also demonstrate how you are taking responsibility for your share of the stress in the relationship. And by the way, the more you practice declining stress conversations, the easier it becomes!

Q: What am I supposed to be doing in that fifteen-minute break?

A: This is your cool-down period. Its purpose is to lower your stress hormones and avoid what is an escalating situation. Ideally, you could use this time to go for a short walk or run which helps the body down-regulate the allostatic system. Alternatively, you can just take yourself into another room, even the bathroom, anywhere you can shut the door and be by yourself. While you are alone, you may want to write down how you are feeling and identify what part of your body was triggered.

Q: How will I know if my partner is ready to have a constructive conversation?

A: If your partner is still steaming over your refusal to continue an ongoing stress conversation, it is definitely not the right time. It may be best for you wait. Let your partner come to you and say, "Okay, I'm ready—I'm open to having that talk now." If you need to leave your home while he or she cools down, it may be best talk on the phone before you have a face-to-face discussion.

Q: How do I know if I was triggered by my stressful day or my phantom stressors?

A: While you are taking your fifteen-minute cool down, take a look at the Logosoma trigger chart below. If you find that you are too stressed out to respond accurately to the questions, hold off until you are able to do so.

SHARON AND KEVIN: WHAT CONVERSATION ARE YOU REALLY IN?

Many people do not realize that there are at least eight people in every relationship: you, your partner, both mothers and fathers, and two of what I call two *little me*. Your *little me*, often referred to as the inner child, is a sense of yourself housed in the emotional memories from your past. Your little me never grow up. In fact, little me is like a phantom stressor in that anything in the present that reminds your little me of a past emotional experience, positive or negative, can trigger childlike feelings. For example, these childlike feelings may include secure dependency, magical wonderment, joyful surprise or unresolved conflicts, insecure attachments, repressed grief, buried anger, or irrational fears.

When you have been triggered by a stress conversation and are about to go into fight, flight, or freeze mode, it is up to you to figure out what you are responding to. Was it something dangerous or hurtful uttered by someone in your present or are you reacting to a critical parent from your past? You need to ask yourself: What conversation am I in? Who am I really angry at? Is my response appropriate to the current crisis? In Sharon's case, she was able to figure out she was still intimidated by her critical mother and felt invisible to her dismissive father. Answering hard questions like these caused Sharon to realize she was reacting to Kevin as if he were a critical parent, not the adult man she loved.

THE LOGOSOMA TRIGGER GUIDE

I developed the logosoma trigger guide to simplify the discovery of what conversation you are really in. As you fill in the chart, answer the four questions as openly and honestly as possible. Take a look at the responses of Sharon's chart below and let it act like a guide.

While the logosoma trigger chart will help sort out the underpinnings of your responses, it will also help later on as you approach steps 2 and 3 of Logosoma Brain Training: refocus and reflect.

Sharon says, "I've Been Triggered!" and asks "What Conversation Am I Really In?

What Is the Feeling?	What Is Happening Now?	What Is the Memory?	Who Am I Really Angry At?
Clammy hands, stiff neck, churning stomach, racing heart, etc.	*My husband teased me when I asked "What's for dinner?"*	*As a kid, I hated dinnertime. My mother was so demanding; she never did anything. I always had to set the table and get dinner together before dad got home, or he'd blow a gasket. I hated her for it.*	*My mother—she never cared what I was feeling. I always felt invisible around her. And I hated having to be so responsible. It was up to me to make sure dad didn't blow his top. I'm not really angry at Kevin. I'm just as tired and hungry as he is.*

Now take a look at the blank sample chart provided for your personal trigger responses. In the first column, record your feelings as soon as you have been triggered. Next, ask yourself what event in the present caused your trigger to be activated and record it in column two. Columns three and four are more difficult. If you have any trouble answering these questions, take some time to reflect and search your memories for associations. The answers may be both surprising and enlightening.

Your turn: "I've Been Triggered!" and "What Conversation Am I Really In?"

What Is the Feeling?	What Is Happening Now?	What Is the Memory?	Who Am I Really Angry At?

I want you to return to the logosoma trigger chart whenever you have been triggered. Please be diligent about filling it in. Each time you fill in the chart, you are training new brain circuits that will lay a foundation for new habits. Keep a journal of when you have been triggered. It will help you keep tabs on the progress of your emerging self-awareness. It this way, you will begin to distinguish your personal phantom stressors from the general stress of everyday life.

Filling out the logosoma trigger chart will help you to calm down. It will provide you with a log of *when* your stressors appear and start to reveal just *what* triggers your closet of phantoms. I train my patients to distinguish the two cases by using the words *pain* and *suffering*.

Pain and Suffering: What's the Difference?

I use the term *pain* to designate three different categories of physical distress: tissue damage, separation or loss, and shame. Our brains are wired for the pain of tissue damage and for attachment, with its pain of separation and loss. Shame, however, is taught. We learn shame and humiliation as children through negative assessments. Some call it blame, "dissing" (dismissing), put downs, criticisms, devaluing, and scolding.

No two people have the identical shame profile. Even identical twins experience shame differently. Although they share the same DNA, their life experience is not exactly the same; hence, their behavior is unique. And as we all know, the negative assessment that causes shame is only momentary, but the feeling of shame can last a lifetime.

I use the term *suffering* to designate an irrational fear of pain in the future that triggers a stress response in the present. You may call it worry or anxiety. But let us be clear: your body's stress circuits are triggered as if your body were in real pain. There is no enemy hitting you on the head or taking some precious object away from you, but your stress hormones have been triggered just the same. Your body is looking to fight or flee from an imaginary enemy. This is what the irrational side of suffering is all about. And suffering is stressful.

The fear of pain in the future or remembering pain from past is potent enough to trigger a stress response. The memory of yesterday's pain can actually amplify the fear of tomorrow. This is especially true if you have had a serious accident, lost a loved one, or if you were continually shamed as a child. Excessive criticism during childhood can leave one's sense of self extremely vulnerable to shame triggers later on. People who have suffered excessive criticism often become obsessive and compulsive perfectionists as adults.

BRAIN SCAN: UNMASKING INSECURE ATTACHMENTS FROM THE PAST

Why is it important for you to discover what conversation you are really in?

In adult intimacy, everyone can feel the childlike emotions of vulnerability and dependency from time to time. When events in the present trigger emotions from the past—as with phantom stressors—the brain can become flooded with cumulative feelings of fear and anger. Insecure attachments that develop in the early years from overly stressed mother-infant bonding or traumatic events from the past can compound your daily stresses and affect your emotional connections with people in the present. Managing this emotional duality of present-day stress with past phantom stressors is a formidable task. But when you make these distinctions, you begin to strengthen the security of your emotional bonds.

When you are part of an insecure attachment, you may find yourself acting and feeling like a child or a hostage. When chronic stress invades your relationships, it can re-trigger cycles of unresolved conflict and insecurity from your past and set the stage for dysfunctional behavior in the present. I call this chronic state of stress in your relationship connections a *hostage relationship*. Although there are similarities, the commonly used term codependency does not reflect the chronic stress physiology of a hostage relationship, where each brain becomes hostage to stress hormones. Normal brain function and social interaction are impaired. The relationship becomes stuck. When the individual leaves the hostage relationship and their body begins to down-regulate, their brain function returns to normal.

Your limbic system, one of the oldest parts of your brain, records the emotional scripts of your personal dramas of love, security and power during early childhood attachment patterns with your parents. In adult intimacy, it is your idealized hopes and expectations that drive who you become attached to. But these lofty ideals must compete with the mostly unconscious fears of the unbearable relationship disappointments of the past, your phantom stressors. Unless we learn to identify the emotional undercurrents of stressors inherited from our past attachments, we risk partnership disaster in the present. Unfortunately, the human capacity to suffer is hard-wired into our brain. Suffering evolved as a survival mechanism to override reflective thought during periods of chronic stress. You cannot stop to reflect on the full moon if you have irrational fears of what is lurking in the darkness! Your Logosoma Brain Training will help you successfully overcome your instinct to suffer during stressful episodes of your life. You will be able to conquer your irrational fear of the future so you can stop worrying about tomorrow—and live for today.

Q&A—QUESTIONS FROM MY PATIENTS

Q: What if I can't identify the feeling of stress in my body? What if it just feels like dread, anger or resentment?

A: You may not be able to locate the stress in a certain part of your body, particularly when your emotions are running high. However, a sense of dread, anger, or resentment is often visible in your facial expressions. So take a look in the mirror. And remember those expressions!

Q: When I'm triggered, not just one but several memories often come to the surface. How do I know which is the "real" phantom stress?

A: There may be many phantom stressors for any single stress trigger. But at this stage, it is not so important to analyze which is more important. It is much better to acknowledge that you have been triggered and you must now *refuse* the stress invitation. This will open the possibility to *refocus* your attention away from the stress trigger later on.

Q: I had an extremely difficult childhood. When I try to figure out which conversation I'm in, I have lots of possibilities to choose from. Should I write down as many as I can remember?

A: Yes, creating a list of your phantom stressors is a good practice. Get to know your demons, all of them. The more you are conscious of them, the less likely they will be to take your brain hostage.

HELEN: FROM PHANTOM STRESS TO LEARNED HELPLESSNESS

A couple of months after I first worked with Helen and her partner, she came in alone and reported, "Alan is just not cooperating with your Logosoma Training. I'm starting to feel it's not worth it for me to go it alone."

Although I told her "going it alone" would benefit her in the long run, she called it quits. Not surprising, however, Helen returned with more serious complaints a year later.

"I'm so irritable now; I'm just not able to focus on my job. Although I'm sleeping a lot, I'm still tired all the time," Helen told me. Her eyes had dark circles around them. They looked scared all the time, like a deer in the headlights. "I've practiced dance and tai chi for enough years to teach a master class at my center. But I'm still so afraid that I'm not good enough. It's crazy! I feel like my boss is just waiting for me to mess up so she can fire me. I am so full of doubt about things that I used to feel so confident about. Alan doesn't even seem to notice how stressed out I am. He's so preoccupied with getting a promotion at work, he travels all the time. I hardly see him anymore. And when he's home, I seem to have very little connection with him. He seems to be losing interest in me, yet I'm too afraid to speak up. I think he might leave me if I complain. I feel like I'm sinking out of existence."

Helen's story illustrates the extreme damage on the body and mind caused by chronic stress.

BACK STORY: NO ESCAPE FROM A CRITICAL MOTHER

Helen felt helplessly locked in a chronically stressful marriage, flooded with self-doubt and terrified of being abandoned. She had learned her helplessness as a child in the insecure attachment of her mother-infant relationship. Early life with her mother, her primary caregiver, had been critical in shaping Helen's brain's neural structure for intimacy. A self-centered, nonempathic, and even emotionally abusive mother laid the groundwork in her brain for a starring role as the submissive wife to a self-centered husband. In childhood, Helen's brain learned that there was no escape from mother, but that no matter how stressful their relationship became, mother was needed. Helen had internalized the hostage role from this chronically stressed intimate relationship. She could not flee from her mother, nor could she flee from her husband. Her allostatic load had taken the form of a self-sabotaging behavior pattern called *learned helplessness*. Identified in 1965 in laboratory animals, this condition results from extreme chronic stress and leads the animal to just give up on life, even when escape is possible.

Helen's tai chi practice probably kept her sane enough to return to consultation, but it could not protect her from the chronic stress of her neglectful husband.

We are taught from childhood that suppressing emotion is a successful social skill, and indeed, this is a life-long practice that has many adaptive benefits, like good manners and social connectedness. Helen's situation is extreme. Her case demonstrates there are times when the cost of such emotional suppression is too high, both in physiological and psychological terms. In fact, research on emotional expression demonstrates that if you hide your feelings (the smile-and-wave response your mother taught you), your stress goes up and lasts longer.

UNLEARNING LEARNED HELPLESSNESS

Helen needed to unlearn her helplessness. So we trained rigorously desensitize her amygdala to Alan's negative assessments whether they were explicit or implicit. By the repetitive drilling of a single response, Helen learned to refuse the stress invitation implicit in Alan's many put downs or dismissals. She was able to stand up fearlessly to her husband using a simple but powerful deflection of his attacks: "I've been triggered, and I need some time alone. Please do not bother me." Newly empowered, Helen began to follow both her Logosoma coaching and her wish to separate from Alan. The writing was on the wall a year ago when he declared, "I don't have any problems. And I don't need therapy—you do!"

HELEN: REFUSING YOUR OWN STRESS INVITATION

It is not always your partner who triggers your phantom stress circuits. More often than not, you invite yourself into a stress conversation. Helen told me that after learning to *refuse* the stress conversation with Alan, "It hit me that I was continually accepting my own stress invitations without even knowing it. I was in the supermarket playing an argument over and over in my mind I'd had with Alan two weeks ago. Suddenly I realized how angry I was at all his put-downs and dismissals of me. I became incredibly agitated and had a stomach ache. I reminded myself of those crazy people on the streets talking to themselves, as if they were still trying to get some closure on an old unfinished argument. The only difference was I wasn't doing it out loud."

Helen's perception led her to apply her Logosoma Brain Training to herself. "When I catch myself reliving the injustice, no matter where I am, I say out loud, 'Stop!' Then to myself I say, '*I refuse this stress invitation. No one is badgering me; no one is making negative assessments. I'm safe.*'" At that point, she refocused on her next activity, in this case, lunch with a friend. Within minutes, she felt her negative mood and tense muscles melt away.

HOW DO YOU FEEL? WHAT IS HAPPENING IN YOUR BRAIN?

At this point in your training, you have learned to identify stress invitations and to say no. You are now taking time out to down-regulate your allostatic system. It might feel a little scary—change usually does. Paradoxically, so does ending your sense of being the wounded party, a victim or hostage. You have started the process of brain change. By saying "I've been triggered," you are confronting the bottom-up stress messages from your body with a top-down message from the executive area of your prefrontal cortex. You are telling your body to stop so your brain can get more information before you freeze, fight, or flee. You are opening up new circuits, taming your amygdala, your fear center, and beginning to trust your thinking cortex.

You are now ready to refocus your attention away from the grip of a phantom stressor to the present.

Chapter 6

Step 2: Refocus Your Attention

> *Consciousness is more than perceiving and knowing;*
> *it is knowing that you know.*
> —**Jeffrey M. Schwartz, MD**

In step 1, refuse the stress conversation, you learned to identify a stress response in your body by paying attention to bottom-up sensations. When these signs emerge, you can now say "I've been triggered!" Identifying when you have been triggered is the first step to liberating yourself from being a hostage to stress. Armed with a new awareness, you now have the option to decline all forms of stress conversations, whether in your head or with another person. By taking fifteen to thirty minutes to cool down, the nonconscious startle message that triggered your phantom stressors has time to get to your cortex, the conscious part of your brain. This allows you to make a more thorough assessment of just what really triggered you *before* you begin to freeze, fight, or flee and lose your ability to think and act rationally. By cooling down, your body can begin to metabolize the cascade of stress hormones in your system, helping you to down-regulate and think more clearly.

You are now ready for step 2, refocus your attention. Refocusing your attention will help you create an opportunity for your brain to reframe your perception of your personal stress triggers, disarming their insidious effects. By neutralizing your phantom stressors, you will be able to leave the grip of your past behind, recover your attention in the present and become reconnected to the joys of being alive.

Your Refocus Slogan: Validate, Empathize, and Discuss (The VED Script)

The number one trigger of phantom stress is negative assessments. I have developed a universal solvent to help you dissolve them. I call it the VED script (validate, empathize, and discuss). Using this three-part technique will help calm your brain after a stress trigger and lead you to refocus your attention on more self-respecting actions. You will be able to resist making the stress-driven, impulsive, destructive comments, or actions that automatically follow anything you perceive as a negative assessment. So after saying "I've been triggered," and taking a break to cool down, I want you to start developing one of the most important Logosoma Brain Training skills:

Validate: "I can see how you can say that."
Empathize: "I'm sorry you feel that way."
Discuss: "I'm open to discuss it now or later."

This script allows you to respond to any negative assessment, whether it is grounded or ungrounded. With the VED script, you can deflect any of your personal phantom stressors—or a here and now stress—and stay cool. By validating, you are reframing what you perceive as a *negative assessment* into *another person's opinion*, giving it a more neutral charge. Validating does not mean you have to agree with them. You are merely showing respect for their point of view. By empathizing with your critics, you demonstrate concern for their emotions. By declaring your openness to discuss the issue, you invite the recovery of joint attention and connectedness to solve the issues at hand.

When you are in a work situation, staying cool under fire is often achieved by suppressing emotions, like anger, frustration, and fear. It is often inappropriate to discuss what triggered your personal phantom stress on the job with your coworkers. Most phantom stress triggers at work can be resolved alone or outside the workplace with some reflection. We will discuss how to use reflection to navigate stress in chapter 7 with step 3.

Suppressing your emotions at work is one thing, but who wants to do this when you come home? You need to get out of uniform after a hard day at work. You want to come home to a safe sanctuary, a place where you do not need to be vigilant, where you can be your true self and connect with the people you love. When you are dealing with intimate relationships at home, you need a mechanism other than suppression. When you are triggered by a negative assessment from a loved one, rather than from a critical boss, you may impulsively retaliate by saying hurtful things you do not intend. The VED script is your weapon for neutralizing these destructive, knee-jerk reactions.

BRAIN SCAN: REBOOTING YOUR FRONTAL ATTENTIONAL NETWORK

The frontal lobes (prefrontal cortex or PFC) of your brain house the attentional network; this is the part of your brain where clear thinking, decision making, evaluating, future planning, and reflection are processed. The PFC is connected to all parts of the brain. The PFC's job is to pay attention to what is occurring in the present. When you perceive something as threatening, for example, a word, a tone of language, or a facial expression, your senses trigger the amygdala. It starts a flood of neuronal and hormonal changes that send a message to your body through the low road: "You're in danger!" Your brain's ancient default mode of survival behavior takes over your actions and dictates that you need to fight, flee, or freeze. The amygdala sends an overriding message to the PFC: "We don't have time for analytic and reflective thinking right now. I need to get this body out of danger!"

In a flash, your amygdala mobilizes your body to respond to the perceived threat. In doing so, it shuts down your frontal attentional network just as quickly. This is the point where your capability for thinking straight or carrying on a rational conversation vanishes.

We are not slaves to our stress physiology, however. There is another path. The high road from the amygdala to the prefrontal cortex opens the way for you to learn to recognize your stress triggers. Your brain's high road links with a complex network of circuits designed to learn new, more adaptive ways to deal with old stressors. These PFC networks help you assess the value of choices that confront you. They also help you quickly reframe a negative experience into a positive one, known as *reversal learning*. The PFC networks include exotic frontiers of your brain: the orbitofrontal cortex, parahippocampal region, ventral striatum, and other regions that also connect to the hippocampus, the structure involved in making new memories, in spatial orientation, and in emotional regulation. The orbitofrontal cortex (OFC) can override the startle response triggered by the amygdala. The OFC achieves this by activating the hippocampus, the part of the brain that sends the "all clear" message to the body, telling it to stop the elevated production of stress hormones.

Anyone familiar with cardiopulmonary resuscitation (CPR) knows that an important part of the training is learning how to remain calm during a crisis so you can perform its life-saving steps. Like CPR training, step 2, refocus your attention, will prepare you in advance to recover and maintain the connection with your attentional network during a stress response. In this way, you will not lose the ability to think clearly when the stress hormones start flooding into your body. You will "keep your cool" and stay focused.

You have now recovered your attentional network through grounded assessments of what is actually happening to you. You have taken your fifteen-minute break. Now you are ready to go back to the situation that triggered you. Let us see how Laura uses her Logosoma Brain Training to help navigate her phantom stress with Rob to recover joint attention with him.

LAURA AND ROB: WHAT IS JOINT ATTENTION?

Laura and Rob love playing tennis together. It helps them unwind and provides them with an opportunity to chat.

Laura recalled, "Once we were practicing our moves with a warm-up volley and talking about a vacation. When Rob suggested a specific hotel he wanted to go to, I suddenly felt overwhelmed by a sense of dread. My attention was hijacked off the tennis court. I felt like I was fifteen again, thrown back twenty years to a horrible summer experience with my family at that same hotel. My hands began to sweat and my ears were ringing. I froze and the ball went right by me. I wanted to throw my racket at Rob for reminding me of that experience and run off the court. I hardly heard Rob when he called out, 'Hey, what's up? Where did you go?'"

Laura and Rob lost joint attention. The joy they shared in their connection through their tennis volley and vacation planning had just been derailed by one of Laura's phantom stressors.

THE POWER TO REFOCUS: FREE WON'T, NOT FREE WILL

In step 2, refocus your attention, you will be rebooting your frontal attentional network which has just started to crash as a result of a stress response. Laura's teen memories of a nightmare hotel have taken her eye off the ball. And now the game/conversation cannot proceed. Her body is following the stress reaction instead of playing tennis or making vacation plans with Rob.

Logosoma Brain Training, however, has empowered Laura to say no to her body's stress response. She has the option to save the rational, observing part of the prefrontal cortex from being swamped by her stress hormones. She has learned the skills in step 1 to refuse the stress conversation and will use step 2 to refocus her attention from the grip of her phantom stressor back to the game and conversation. She knows that she has only a brief window of opportunity for her brain to refocus attention. This window of opportunity allows her to exercise *free won't*.

BRAIN SCAN: 550 MILLISECONDS TO REFOCUS

Common sense tells us that will power is what prevents us from overeating, smoking or lashing out at someone when you are angry. Neuroscientists, however, have demonstrated that will power or free will may be illusory. Consider when a smoker says, "I know I should quit, but I'm just going to have one more cigarette." Free will enables the smoker to take a final smoke. But freedom rings hollow in this case. To exercise real freedom, the smoker has another option: they can veto the impulse and say no to the urge.

Scientists have measured an approximately 550-millisecond (half a second) gap between an impulse and when it is acted upon. During this gap, there is an option to veto the impulse—this is when you exercise *free won't*.

For instance, you think, "I want another piece of chocolate." Before you actually think, "I want it," your hand is set in motion. By the time you consciously register, "I want it," you have already reached out for another piece. But you still have half a second to veto the impulse, to choose not to grab another piece of chocolate cake and exercise *free won't*. Exercising free won't takes lots of practice. Anyone who has ever tried to change an unhealthy habit like smoking knows just how hard it is to say no to such a deeply rooted urge.

LAURA AND ROB AND STEP 2: RECOVERING JOINT ATTENTION

Laura and Rob have had enough Logosoma Brain Training to recognize that keeping their brains safe from disabling stress hormones is the best route to a deep, intimate connection. They know how to identify when they have been triggered and how to work as a team to recover their joint attention.

After Laura was triggered into re-experiencing her teenage vacation trauma on the tennis court, she exercised her free won't by telling Rob, "I've been triggered." She walked off the court to calm her amygdala. After walking around a bit, she took some deep breaths and started shifting her attention.

Laura recalls, "I knew that I was terrified by the thought of going back to that hotel. In my Logosoma Brain Training, I learned to say no to the freeze/fight/flight urges of my fears and yes to my wishes. By telling myself *'I'm not going back to that hotel ever again,'* I was able to calm myself down. I could regulate my amygdala and reassure little Laura, the traumatized fifteen-year-old, that I would protect her."

Once Laura soothed herself with this self-respecting thought, she could return to talk to Rob. Their number one agenda was to recover joint attention, not resume their volley or discuss their vacation.

Rob remembered his refocus technique: validate, empathize, and discuss. "Laura, I understand that you needed to stop playing. I'm sorry you're feeling that way. And I'm here for you if you want to discuss anything."

Rob told me he felt abandoned in that moment. He felt as if he had done something wrong to hurt Laura. But his training kicked in. He was able to use the VED script to help protect him, to stay cool long after Laura declared she had been triggered. The slogan reaffirmed he did not need to go and rescue Laura. Nor was he being abandoned. "I've been triggered," is the couple's cue to follow the Logosoma drill. Rob's role in the drill is to be available and ready for a conversation if and when Laura is ready. In the past, the tables were turned. It was Rob who had blown his cool when he felt Laura "abandoned" him, a phantom stressor from his own past.

No conversation, no relationship, no listening, or turn-taking activity between two people can exist without joint attention. Disruptions in joint attention derail connectedness. By recovering joint attention, you are showing an openness to accept responsibility for triggering others and a willingness to refocus your attention to reconnect with your ability to communicate. This is where you learn and practice listening to yourself, showing up honestly, validating your own feelings, and sharing concerns about confusion, anger, and fear. In my work with couples and families, I encourage practice conversations to reassure everyone that even the most intense emotions can be discussed without destructive results.

For now, the critical message is: *refocus your attention from the grip of your past stressors to recover joint attention;* this is the essential practice for connectedness in your relationships.

LAURA AND ROB: FROM PHANTOM STRESS TO ADAPTIVE CONVERSATION

What is an adaptive conversation? An adaptive conversation is a shared narrative experience. Two people with joint attention focus on a single issue or problem, taking turns and sharing until they resolve it. When each partner communicates their true thoughts and feelings about certain issues or problems, they deepen their trust and respect for each other, thereby strengthening their emotional bonds.

Laura and Rob's tennis practice illustrates the dynamics of an adaptive conversation derailed and recovered. They started their volleying and vacation planning with excellent joint attention, taking turns both with their bodies hitting the tennis ball and in language with their conversation about a vacation. They were not playing to win or lose. The goal of an adaptive conversation is to continue the turn-taking until there's some kind of resolution. If the ball goes off the court, as it did for Laura and Rob, they need to recover it and return to the volley—two brains, one ball, joint attention.

Once Laura recovered her composure, she was able to sit down with Rob on the bench next to the court and share her story about the hotel. "It is very hard for me to say what I feel," Laura began, "because the emotions are so intense. It feels like I was there yesterday. When I was fifteen, I was taking tennis lessons with the hotel pro, a young guy about twenty-two. I guess I was flirting a bit and he took it as an invitation. Although I tried to refuse his advances, he ended up forcing himself on me. To make things worse, he threatened to tell my parents that it was I who had seduced him if I dared tell anyone. I was paralyzed with fear and shame. Of course, I didn't tell a soul. I suppressed the incident until now."

Rob listened to Laura attentively. He held her as she cried. "Let's leave the past behind," he whispered, "and get back to having some serious fun in the present!" After drying her tears, they got back onto the court and did just that.

Laura later told me, "Rob was great. He didn't try to rescue me like he used to. He didn't take it as another abandonment either. He just stayed there and comforted me. It was all I needed at that moment."

With each turn in an adaptive conversation, you express your feelings and thoughts about the issue at hand. You listen and empathize with your partner. With practice, you enhance your emotional communication skills and empower your partnership to handle almost any topic, no matter how stressful.

EMOTION: BETTER TO EXPRESS THAN SUPPRESS

I stress the necessity for being honest with yourself and your partner for one simple reason—honest emotional expression resolves stress better than suppressing your emotions. With emotional suppression, you are holding back, denying what you feel. However, your stress hormones continue to escalate. The point of down-regulating your allostatic system is to take yourself out of a situation in which you feel threatened so you can refocus your attention away from the grip of the past. This will help you to start moving toward wish-driven behavior instead of acting out fear-driven behavior. The point is you have a choice. Suffering the ravages of stress is optional! Once you have identified that your enemy is actually inside you in the form of a lurking phantom stressor and not outside you, as in the case of your loving partner, you can choose to say no to your ancient stress circuitry and survival hormones.

We all need, however, to suppress our emotions from time to time for the purposes of social adaptation. If everyone decided to express their entire emotional life in public, there would be no civilization. Our capacity for inhibiting our emotional urges helps us form meaningful connections, trust, and respect for each other, the fabric of all successful social systems. But when the suppression of your feelings becomes excessive and habitual, a false self can develop. You may find yourself turning into a people-pleaser, telling white lies above and beyond ordinary social politeness. Over the course of our lifetime, we are continually performing a balancing act—when to express our emotions and when to hold them in.

There is another, more insidious side to suppressing your feelings. Doing so can take years off of your life. Cardiology researchers found that female heart attack victims who habitually suppressed their opinions in conflicts with their spouses were four times more likely to die during the post-heart attack period than those who spoke up. And women who smile when they are actually fuming inside are in danger of raising their level of stress hormones to chronic levels. These hormones (among them cortisol, norepinephrine, and epinephrine) can, in turn, lead to the development of coronary heart disease.

The path you are making in the Logosoma Brain Training uses words (logos) to identify feelings arising from emotional states in the body (soma). Practicing adaptive conversations with your partner to recover joint attention empowers you to speak honestly about your pain. With repeated experiences of recovering trust, respect, and creativity, you will both be ready for a deeper communion with your own personal truth through mindful awareness.

Q&A—QUESTIONS FROM MY PATIENTS

Q: I'm not sure what I'm supposed to refocus on?

A: Refocusing involves effort: a shift of your attention *away* from a stress trigger, especially a phantom stressor, and *toward* a safe action and context. The first aim of refocusing is to down-regulate your allostatic system after the stress trigger, to "chill out." The best way to do this is to engage both your attention and your body in an action that makes you feel safe. I often recommend that people make a list of things to do when they are triggered, like a fire drill, so you do not have to think something up in the middle of your stress trigger. For example, my patients have come up with a number of activities that work for them including: listening to music on a portable music player, reading a good book that can be carried, taking a walk, drawing on a sketch pad, writing down their feelings, and meditating on their breathing.

Q: What if I'm still feeling angry and hurt five minutes after saying "I've been triggered?"

A: Take another break and continue your refocusing effort until your emotions subside. The amount of time you spend is less important than the physiologic recovery from your body's stress response. Whatever time it takes is worth it. You will decrease your stress hormones and recover your emotional composure.

Q: My husband triggers me way too often and he's just not open to discussing it. What do I do?

A: When you return from your fifteen-minute break after saying "I've been triggered," you need to be prepared to delay the gratification of regaining joint attention with your husband. Ideally, you will be calm enough to say, "Are you ready to have this conversation now or should we have it later?" This means you have to prepare yourself for him to say no. If he does, your follow up can be "I'm open to have this conversation with you whenever you are ready."

Q: Oftentimes when I'm trying to express my feelings I temporarily freeze up in midsentence. Impatient with the pause in the conversation, the person I'm talking to ends up interrupting me before I finish what I wanted to say. How can I prevent this?

A: Your insecurity in self-expression may be rooted in childhood experiences of shame or shyness. By learning a simple, self-respecting phrase, "Excuse me, but I wasn't finished with my thought. May I continue?" you will create a newfound sense of respect for yourself—and gain some from your listener.

Q: My angry outbursts have become so bad, I'm losing respect for myself—and so is everyone else. Can you help me gain control of my quick temper?

A: Absolutely. Recovering self-respect depends on recovering your connection to your brain's frontal attentional network, the control center of your calm, clear thinking. This is what the refocus step in Logosoma Brain Training is all about. When your brain is a hostage of phantom

119

stressors born from feelings of resentment and self-pity from your past, your behavior will be driven by an impulsive, childlike fear and anger in the present. Learning to *refuse* the stress trigger and *refocus* your attention is the beginning of recovering your self-respect and ability to self-regulate your emotions. Some call it anger management. I call it self-parenting.

Q: I'm in a relationship where I feel we have nothing but contempt left for each other. What do I do?

A: Even though you still live together, you are emotionally separated. If both of you want to salvage your connection, this is probably the time to get professional help. Do not pretend everything is fine. You must both agree to accept the truth of your situation and act like respectful roommates. This is not the time to move out. But you need to accept and respect your mutual need for emotional distance from each other. You must now let go of any expectations of your partnership. Only by accepting that you are separated can you begin to recover some dignity and civility with each other, as if you were total strangers. Eventually, you may get interested in a closer relationship with your "roommate," or you may decide to move out.

BRAIN SCAN: FROM NONCONSCIOUS BODY STATES TO NAMING FEELINGS

Paying attention to feelings and naming them is one of the greatest features evolution has given your brain. More than 200 million years of evolution and the development of 40 billion neurons in your prefrontal cortex (PFC) provide you with an elegant circuitry for modulating behavior beyond the survival imperatives of fight/flight. Logosoma Brain Training takes full advantage of your brain's civilizing, resilient circuitry in the PFC. By using your brain's high road for making assessments of the here and now in order to *refuse* triggers, you can *refocus* away from the fear sensations in your body and reframe your perception of the stress trigger. The reframed perception opens the way to act more appropriately, whatever the situation may be. Sensations of fear experienced through your body's sensory nervous system send bottom-up messages to your brain. When you feel threatened as a result of a smell, a taste, a touch, a sight, or a sound, your brain gets the message that danger is near. It responds by sending startle messages back to parts of your body such as the muscles, internal organs, and immune system. Virtually every cell in your body is mobilized for survival through chemical messengers in the blood (hormones), and electrochemical messages through your nervous system (neurotransmitters). The message is "Beware!"

Any of your five senses can send startle messages to your brain, causing your body to react instinctively. For example, when you sniff the smell of sour milk in your refrigerator, you reflexively recoil in disgust. Putting on your summer shoes, you step on a small sharp pebble and the pain makes you literally jump out of your shoes. Hearing the sound of a braking train, the high-pitched screeching sound of metal on metal, makes you instantly plug up your ears. The point is that no matter which sensory system sends the warning message, your stress response triggers you to react instantaneously.

Remember, too, that your brain can be triggered by *distortions* of sensory data. If the taste of the food, the sound of a tune from your childhood, or any other sensation reminds you of painful past experiences, your body will respond with a freeze/fight/flight response just as if it were actually threatened in the present. Your brain's take on the safety or risks of any social situation will thus determine how you express your emotions. All of your relationships, whether they are with a partner, your family, friends, and coworkers are perpetually monitored by nonconscious brain circuits that evaluate the safety or danger in any situation.

Logosoma Brain Training helps you identify these circuits as the essential fabric in your social connectedness. By accepting the fact that both here-and-now stresses and phantom stressors can trigger your amygdala, you will be able to distinguish between the two with practice. The good news is that your PFC can learn to reframe the triggering experience delivered through the high road to your PFC. By refocusing your attention, you can reframe the trigger, and modulate and override your inappropriate stress reactions. Neuroscientific research has validated that mindful awareness, one of the most powerful tools your brain has to regulate your emotions, can be learned. I use the term mindful awareness to include both the reflective mental processes of psychotherapy and the techniques of ancient meditation.

In chapter 7, you will learn the fundamental techniques of mindful awareness. With practice, you will reap its immeasurable benefits to your health and well-being.

Chapter 7

STEP 3: REFLECT TO CONNECT: BECOMING YOUR AUTHENTIC SELF

Those who cannot remember the past are condemned to repeat it.

—George Santayana

Are you secure in being yourself? Do you feel connected with your body? Are you showing up as who you really are in your relationships? Are they meaningful to you? What stresses you out the most: your relationships, your job, or where you live? Do you stress yourself out? What are you afraid of? What do you want? These are some of the most fundamental but difficult questions we ask ourselves at some point during the course of our lives. I will help you find the answers. But although I can act as your guide, I cannot answer the questions for you. In fact, no one else can because the answers lie within you. In step 3, I will ask you to make a major shift of your attentional focus. Rather than identifying conditions outside yourself like triggers or stress conversations, I will ask you to start reflecting on what is within.

The essence of step 3 in Logosoma Brain Training is mindful awareness. With reflection, you turn the focus of your attention inward. The act of reflection directly connects you with your physical, emotional and mental self. With reflection, you will gain a deeper understanding of the story you are living in. All your hopes, fears, needs, and desires will emerge when you reflect to connect.

To one degree or another, phantom stress has affected your body, your relationships, and your career. The first step in repairing the damage done is to start re-scripting the part of your personal story of Me that was written under the influence of phantom stress. You will start by getting to know your true self better. Step 3 of Logosoma Brain Training is done by you and you alone, helping you become as mindfully aware of your inner life as possible. Eventually, the reflective skills you develop can be practiced in all of your relationships. In chapter 8, you will learn to create your story of We and have serious fun with others, but first you must look inward. Let us begin the private journey of reflection.

REFLECTION: WHAT IS THE PAYOFF?

The fruits of reflection can be discovered by your answer to three fundamental questions.

Who am I?

What does it all mean?

What am I doing here?

These three questions spontaneously emerge as the teen brain develops the capacity for abstract thinking. The rapidly developing pubertal brain embarks on the life-long effort to integrate *cognition, emotion, and motivation*, what Joseph LeDoux calls the mental trilogy. Young teens are notorious for their direct opposition to parental or cultural traditions. This is the generation gap that often separates teens from their "you should do it our way" families. Even when the most well-meaning parents assert their opinions and views over a developing teenager, it is quite normal for the teenager to react and rebel first, instead of reflecting. Unskilled at reflection, the teenager is often unable to answer the fundamental three questions that can trigger existential anxiety in the teenage brain. The internally generated stress conversation that develops from the angst can last a lifetime unless the brain's capacity for reflection is further developed and used. Mastering the skill of reflection in adulthood, being able to answer the fundamental three questions and feel the peace of finding your true self, is one of the rewards of getting older and wiser.

The payoff is profound.

Answering *"Who am I?"* establishes a *cognitive* inventory, like looking through childhood pictures, reading diary entries from your childhood, or just recalling your autobiography. The path to discovering your true self will become your ongoing project for life.

"What does it all mean?" is the beginning of an *emotional* exploration leading to the discovery of personal meaning. By distinguishing between your phantom stressors from the past and the real stress in the present, you will begin to develop a deeper personal connection to the clarity of the present moment, a sharpened awareness undistorted by stress hormones.

"What am I doing here?" is a *motivational* question that will help you explore your personal meaning in the context of your relationships to people, places, and things. Empathy, generosity, and selfless attention to others spring from connecting with them in a shared experience, the We experience.

Reflecting on these three questions kindles the integration of cognition, emotion, and motivation for a dynamic, balanced, and resilient body and mind. When you use the tools of focused attention and reflection, you can transform the crippling emotional memories of adverse childhood events into harmless memories of emotion. Reflection reframes the feeling of being a victim of to the stresses of life. By accepting life for what it is, a world full of sickness, poverty, and suffering, you can begin to develop a sense of gratitude for what you actually have. By liberating yourself from being the victim of your phantom stressors, a hostage to the adverse events in your past, you can embrace change, the impermanent nature of life. The ability to reflect will create resilience to all forms of stress, even in a world full of change, where nothing stays the same.

WISH VS. FEAR: THE BATTLE FOR AUTHENTICITY

Two other questions will help you to reflect on ordinary life choices with special attention to personal growth and well being in your relationships.

What am I afraid of?

What are my wishes?

Answering these questions is the beginning of facing your fears, the cause of any avoidant behavior patterns you may have developed. Teasing your fears from your wishes will help you distinguish the narrative written by your phantom stressors, your false self, from who you really are when liberated from the grip of stress, your true self.

The process of answering the questions will give rise to a profound sense of personal meaning. You will begin to accept the stressful fact that no matter how attached you become to anything, life is perpetually changing and impermanent.

FROM INSECURE ATTACHMENT TO FALSE SELF

Do you know what you are afraid of? The answer may be obvious to you, but is more often not. The roots of your core stress triggers, your earliest fears for security, begin in the womb during your mother's pregnancy. Imprinted into your amygdala, they continue to remain under the radar of awareness until after you have been born, through the first three years of childhood. During these early years, the adaptive behaviors you develop through bonding with your mother will lay the foundations for all your future adult attachments.

Do you feel secure in being yourself, or do you worry about pleasing everyone?

Do you feel the need to wear a mask to hide your true feelings?

Psychoanalyst D. W. Winnicott discovered that mothers who fail to meet their infant's need for their expressive gestures to be mirrored with validation give rise to the *false self*. When the *not good enough mother* imposes her own gestures instead of mirroring those of her infant, she creates an insecure attachment with her child. Developing a false self during infancy can have catastrophic consequences on your adult life, often resulting in people-pleasing behaviors and white lies that go far beyond mere social politeness. When the false self governs relationships, it can lead to attitudes of resentment, self-pity, and self-sabotaging behaviors like drug addiction and alcoholism.

For better or for worse, the mother-infant relationship is a complex world of reciprocal emotions and behaviors that will sculpt the stress response circuitry of both mother and infant. The infant will emerge from this developmental choreography with a budding sense of self that is directly intertwined with mother, father, family, and culture.

CONNECTING TO YOUR AUTHENTIC SELF

Although you may feel the presence of your conscious "self," no one has ever identified it as a fixed structure in the brain or body. Your "self" is actually a constantly changing dynamic system of neural networks composed of billions of synaptic connections in your brain. These connections are continuously changing based on the experiences in your life, your attitudes and behaviors, and the memories that you compile from these experiences. Your memories shape the way you see the world. Two types of memories—implicit and explicit—accrue throughout your life. You feel the world by accumulating emotional memories through your implicit memory system. Implicit memory begins forming during fetal brain development. These nonconscious emotional memories from early attachment and adaptation to the environment contribute to your intuition, your "gut feeling." They are stored in the amygdala and body maps of the cortex. Your brain automatically and nonconsciously checks out a person, place, or thing by comparing it to a past experience of danger. Is it safe? Is he or she friendly?

You also assess the world through the conscious memories that have been uploaded through the hippocampus and stored as explicit memories. Explicit memories are retrievable memories of emotion and are more objective. You can choose to recall them or avoid them. For example, if you want to conjure up a memory with sadness, look at a photo of a long-deceased pet from childhood. These nostalgic memories of emotion may bring a tear to your eyes, but they do not trigger the overwhelming shock you had as a child when you saw your dog hit by a car.

Through the ability to reflect, you will gradually become aware of your insecurities, irrational fears, and patterns of avoidance. Of course, no human being is totally free of insecurities in their attachments. But the good news is that the fear and loathing from early insecurity that shaped your synaptic brain connections into a false self can be displaced by new, healthier attitudes. By accepting life as it is, you acknowledge your own limitations to change it and the others around you. This will lead to an attitude of gratitude for all the positive experiences in your life, helping you rewire your brain from avoidant to accepting behavior. Logosoma Brain Training guides you to create new synaptic connections that spring from honest assessments of who you are. By practicing a reflective approach to life, you can actually create new connections between brain circuits that lead to healthy social connections and the experience of living as a true self.

ANSWERING THE THREE FUNDAMENTAL QUESTIONS

Question 1: Who am I? The Path to Your Authentic Self

What are you like when you are your true self? The most important features are your heightened sense of self-awareness and emotional honesty. By accepting who you really are, you become capable of facing your own fears, able to explore the past emotional pains you once avoided. You will develop the ability to give and take constructive criticism, learning how to be opinionated without being judgmental. Being able to transform negative assessments into constructive conversations will make you more appealing to talk to, helping you to develop a healthy sense of mutual respect in all of your relationships. Best of all, you will be able to make the changes in your attitude and behavior to strengthen your connection to yourself and to others.

The importance of becoming your true self cannot be overestimated. No one starts life with an authentic story of a true self. Your earliest stories do not actually start with you, but with your parents, in the dreams they had about the child they wished for, long before you were conceived. No story happens in a vacuum. They are almost always parables of interdependency, linking us with each other, with our history, culture, and environment. Your true story emerges from reciprocal relationships that are dynamic, evolving, and adaptive. The interplay with your parents, families, friends, teachers, culture, and environment shapes the development of your perception of who you really are. Conflict and compromise inform every step of the path toward an authentic self and a true life story.

Do you want to free yourself from the past? Do you want to liberate yourself from the resentments and self-pity that naturally arise from everyday disappointments, insecure attachments, and painful life experiences? Do you want to neutralize the phantom stressors from the past that haunt your present?

The path to your true self is rooted in creating self-respecting action with others. Living in what I call an *authentic Me narrative*, will be the simplest yet most difficult practice of your life. Social interaction is the most complex human activity known to mankind. It may take a lifetime of practice to master it.

HOWARD: PHANTOM STRESS IN A GILDED CAGE

Howard radiates a kind of boyish sadness as he enters my office for his first session. Although he's forty-eight years old, he looks ten years younger. He is married to a loving wife. They have three children, a boy, twelve, and twin girls, nine. Howard owns and operates a thriving business. He has close ties with his parents and a warm relationship with his two sisters. On the surface, his life seems about as close to perfect as anyone might wish for. So what is Howard doing in my office?

Howard begins by telling me how unfulfilled he feels. "I'm ashamed to say it, Dr. Romero. I feel bored with my life, even though I know I shouldn't." Uninspired by his work, Howard is afraid to tell his wife how hollow and pointless his life feels. In turn, she complains that Howard rarely disciplines their children. He just gives them whatever they want.

Howard is a hostage of a false self. He has built a rich life for himself and family. He genuinely loves his wife and children. Most men would feel proud to be as able to give money to their sisters, their children, and their parents. So why is he suffering every day, living in a story deprived of personal meaning? What happened?

BACK STORY: HOWARD'S FEAR OF SAYING NO

Howard's life story can be compressed into the following highlights: energetic as a boy, a cautious risk-taker as a teen, a compassionate young college student, an adventurous young adult, and world traveler; through all this, a loyal son and brother. Later on, Howard settled down and became a devoted husband and father to his children, and his business started taking off. But despite the success story, there has been one glaring theme that recurred over Howard's entire life. He has almost never pursued his own wishes. He sees himself as a victim of circumstance, ruled by the wishes of his parents, his wife, his friends, his children, or whatever life happens to offer him. Being a successful entrepreneur, he took risks, but they were rarely motivated by "I want to do that." He was being merely reactionary and opportunistic rather than purposeful. All of Howard's adventures and experiments seemed to be at the suggestions of other people. Rather than come up with his own ideas and wishes, Howard was motivated by a "Why not?" attitude.

He could not say no to anyone. And he was doing this most of his life without even knowing it.

Howard lived behind the mask of the false self. Not only was he unable to say no to anyone, he could not say yes to himself. Instead, Howard suppressed his feelings and complied with other people's wishes. He did this to please them but suffered, depriving himself of his own true story. Howard lived in stories told by others, by his parent's wishes, his wife's wishes, his children's wishes, his customers' wishes—anyone's wishes but his own.

As a result, Howard was indifferent to the successes in his life. He had no emotional investment motivating his actions. He did everything for others and felt that there was no time left for him. The only time Howard was free to say yes to himself was in his private fantasy life and dreams. It was no surprise to find they were filled with villainous scenarios in which he broke all the rules, acted out against his own morals and betrayed society's ethics and laws. Howard's "evil double" within triggered his phantom stress, the secret sense of shame and guilt he harbored, causing him to develop deadly chronic stress. Left a hostage of his own split self-image, the good Howard lived by the tyranny of "should" and the evil Howard ran amok in fantasy.

Howard was withholding his personal truth. He was terrified of displeasing the people he loved, fearing they would be disappointed or get angry at him. Anger was frightening to Howard, particularly his own anger. He was afraid anger would release his inner demons, making him very, very dangerous. Feeding off his isolation, the chronic stress that Howard endured went undetected by those around him. He lived in a private story of stress. His constant effort to suppress his dark wishes was exhausting. As he had never developed the skills to deal with negative emotions in social situations, Howard simply avoided conflict and confrontation. He was alone, a hostage of his own fear of negative emotion.

HOWARD'S SECRET IN THE GILDED CAGE

Suffering in a void of personal meaninglessness, Howard felt like he was a hostage to his fear of getting angry. He retained his dark secret, *"I'm a fake, a coward,"* and expended huge amounts of energy suppressing negative emotions. Scientists have discovered this suppression actually increases the intensity and duration of your stress response. The allostatic load of Howard's chronic stress had been repeatedly triggered by feelings of shame and guilt for his "evil" thoughts, leaving him with a life that, while rich in material things, feels empty and meaningless.

When Howard began Logosoma Brain Training, he became aware of just how often he withheld his personal truth and how terrified he was of displeasing anyone. As a child, Howard had been moderately hyperactive. He frequently found himself singled out and punished at school as a trouble-making clown. Never malicious or defiant, Howard was seen as an underachiever. Looking back, he may have had attention deficit hyperactive disorder that was never treated. The recurrent experiences of shame and humiliation he experienced at home and school become so ordinary for him that he learned to smile and cover up the sadness and anger he held within. By the time he became a teenager, Howard learned to use his high intelligence to adapt. He figured out how to go underground with his identity. He became a secret dodger of the rules, as opposed to an outwardly rebellious rule-breaker.

As Howard reflected painfully on "little Howard" he discovered a boy with a recurring story about himself: *"I am a bad boy. I am ashamed of myself. My wishes are wrong. If I want friends I must behave to please others."* The hundreds of times Howard had been shunned during grade school became so deeply ingrained in his own lack of self-worth; he became a full-time emotional hostage of shame, unable to indulge in the simplest of his wishes unless he was alone. This result was that the true Howard had to be isolated, disconnected from everyone. In Howard's need to disconnect socially, he lost connections to others and to the world; he lost meaning. In his isolation, Howard's true self found music. He learned to play the piano. It became his private sanctuary, a place where all of his fear, anger, frustration, and insecurity could be expressed secretly. But when Howard started performing, things changed. He began to reconnect socially, a factor that proved to be critical in liberating himself from the grip of phantom stress.

BRAIN SCAN: THE *FRANKENTEEN* BRAIN LEARNS TO REFLECT

Reflection on your true self is not a skill that a child's brain can learn. The ability for abstract reflection and theory-making emerges during adolescent brain development. Howard recalls, "I remember getting really interested in philosophy around sixteen. I had so much anxiety about myself then. I thought that philosophy could answer my questions, but it was hard to understand. I felt fat. My complexion was horrible. I was terrified of girls. My best friend Roy was a pothead from a nearby public school. My parents doted on my sisters, so as long as I made Bs they hardly noticed me. I felt like a freak, an ugly monster."

I refer to these experiences as the *Frankenteen* years. During this critical period, the teen brain grows enormous numbers of synaptic connections, increasing the size of the gray matter of the cortex beyond that of normal adults. Then, from about sixteen until the early 20s, the brain goes through a process of pruning the excess number of synaptic connections. The pruning happens as the result of your experience. The synaptic connections you use are not only retained but strengthened. And the ones you do not use atrophy, wither, and die. The pruning process is one of the most dramatic and important examples of neuroplasticity, the brain's ability to reconfigure its neural networks.

A critical goal during the teen years is to plant the seed of achieving personal meaning through reflection. But this task has some serious natural obstacles! Besides the massive surge in synaptic growth, the Frankenteen brain is driving the budding adult body to experiment. Fueled by sex hormones and a newly developed skill for abstract thinking and the idealization of values like romance and fantasy making, the Frankenteen brain naturally pushes the envelope at every opportunity. In its struggle to claim ownership of the body, the Frankenteen brain creates personal stories of opposition and defiance to parental control and social authority. Risk-taking behaviors are coupled with a sense of immortality and idealization, explaining why pop culture heroes commonly preoccupy the mental and emotional world of teenagers. Frankenteen feels alienated from the security of family, and yet is daunted by challenge of becoming an independent adult. For reflection to gain a foothold and establish a narrative of personal meaning, the Frankenteen must navigate the natural stressors of impulsivity and risk-taking from within, and the controlling world of parents and society from without.

As a teenager, you would have started developing your own view of the world. Your budding identity developed opinions about music, style, and politics that differed to your parents' views. In extreme cases, these opinions lead to rebellion in the form of an oppositional attitude toward the values of your parents and society. If you were encouraged to practice reflective thinking when you were young, you would probably be good at it now. During your teenage life, however, your brain is only beginning to develop the capacity for abstract thinking. Along with making cognitive leaps during this phase of brain development, you also develop a greater skill at *affect regulation*—the ability to reflect abstractly on emotions, to identify feelings, to think them through, and to redirect them to adaptive behaviors in the future.

HOWARD'S FRANKENTEEN DILEMMA

"I was about 16 when Roy and I got stoned on a Saturday and decided to break into the school swimming pool," Howard reflected. "We thought it was wrong for us to be locked out of the pool on weekends. We also thought no one would ever know. We wanted to beat the 'evil' system that locks kids out of the pool on weekends! Of course, we had no clue that there was a security guard on duty, so we got caught. The police became involved and called our parents. I remember my mother's face, an animal-like scowl I'd never seen before. In an ice-cold, slow, low tone she uttered a simple line that still terrifies me to this day: 'This will never happen again!' I don't think I'd ever felt shame so deeply in my life, before or since."

HOWARD: LEARNING RUTHLESS COMPASSION FOR YOURSELF

On the path to his own true narrative, Howard discovered that he had lived most of his life in fear of a phantom stressor. Since the infamous swimming pool episode, all his actions were weighed against the consequences of invoking his mother's cold-hearted anger. Howard's fear of shame had been scripted during early childhood. So, despite his high energy and socially warm temperament as a child, he never got into any serious trouble until the swimming pool break-in. The emotional impact on his developing brain was so powerful that he began a lifelong practice of avoiding any situation that might result in disapproval. His true wishes to take risks were stifled. His secret identity remained active in his fantasy life, where he saw himself as self-centered manipulator, an evil villain, the timeless embodiment of the Frankenteen monster.

To free this fear within, Howard would need to validate himself as a teenager. The incident traumatized his developing sense of himself and discouraged reflection and experimentation. Howard adapted to the swimming pool shame by giving his true self, his personal meaning, a life sentence in a prison of *should*. Many "good" people live under the tyranny of should as a result of traumatic shame during childhood or chronic shaming from controlling parents or society. They live in a world of the conditional, never really able to make decisions based on what they truly feel. The blueprint for Howard's every action had to be to take care of his family and bring no shame to them. "I believed that if I just made lots of money and took care of everyone, then I'd be OK," Howard explained. Howard's once-secure emotional attachment with his family became subverted into a story of financial security. His fear of shame led him into a bad deal with himself; he traded love for money as the source of secure attachment and lost his connection with his wishes, the foundation of his authentic sense of self.

To free himself in the future, Howard needed to cultivate four essential attitudes. It is a simple task, but not necessarily an easy one. Brain science tells us that the more you practice any effort to cultivate a new habit or attitude, the easier it becomes.

The four essential attitudes for finding your true life story are:

- *Acceptance* that your past stressors have held your brain hostage
- *Gratitude* that you can break your old habits by changing the wiring of your brain with regular practice of reflection and meditation
- *Willingness* to practice new attitudes and behaviors that lead to your authentic self and true life story
- *Fearless honesty* to assert your wishes

As Howard became more mindfully aware, he began listening to himself more deeply, particularly to his wishes. By practicing ruthless self-compassion, he finally accepted that although he had been reckless and impulsive as a teenager, he was not an evil person. He saw how the self-imposed prison of *should* offered no parole, no matter how many good deeds he performed for his family.

Howard used the *"Who am I?"* reflection to learn just how his life events triggered his fears of shame over and over. The payoff was liberation and emotional independence. He reported, "I want to bring meaning into my life, so I need to find out what I'm passionate about. I began to realize that I was bored with everything, even the good stuff that I used to enjoy. I was losing interest in sharing, exploring and enjoying the adventure of my life with my wife Barbara and the kids. They used to make me really happy."

If you want to create serious fun, you have to know what excites you, what you find compelling. If you feel unmotivated and lacking in passion, and your purpose in your relationships is driven by should, you are bound to confront a crisis of meaning. If you feel the connection with your family, friends, career, and your environment is not nurturing or stimulating, you need to explore your inner world to enrich and inspire you. The poet Ezra Pound wrote, "What thou love's well is thy true heritage."

FROM REFLECTION TO RELAXATION TO MEDITATION

Ancient mindfulness training strategies work by enhancing your natural ability for reflection by creating the *relaxation response*. The most common technique is to follow your breath or concentrate on an object, a word, a sound, or phrase. I would suggest you begin by sitting in a comfortable position with your eyes slightly closed and concentrate on your breathing. This may be harder than you think. Beginners often find the everyday train of thought breaks their attentional focus after just a few moments. This is totally normal. If this happens, gently return your attention to following your breathing. Gradually, your oxygen consumption decreases, muscles relax, attention sharpens, and a sense of emotional calm pervades.

The workings of the brain can now be scanned and visualized using functional magnetic resonance imaging (fMRI). Brain scans comparing ordinary people with Tibetan Buddhist monks demonstrate that people inclined to dwell in negative emotions display a persistent pattern of activation in the right prefrontal cortex. Prolonged states of negative emotion produce allostatic load leading to chronic stress. This physiology of suffering leaves you much more vulnerable to negative emotions. People with a brighter disposition and positive attitude show a heightened activity in the left prefrontal cortex. The science that validates the hypothesis that meditation alters the resting emotional state of the brain and enhances attentional functioning is still in its infancy. However, an fMRI scan of the brain of a Tibetan lama skilled in meditation showed a baseline activity to the extreme left of the PFC, the "happy zone," well beyond anyone else ever tested.

Armed with this finding, scientists set up an experiment with volunteers from a high-tech company. One group received eight weeks of training in meditation. Another control group received no training at all. All participants also were given flu shots. Seasoned practitioners of meditation will not be surprised by the findings. The group of meditators showed a robust shift in brain activation toward the left PFC (the "happy zone") and also demonstrated a healthier immune response to the flu shot. What this indicates is that the brain training not only enhanced their state of mind, but also strengthened their body's immune system.

Question 2: What Does It All Mean?

Hand in glove with the development of a true self is the reward and benefit derived from one's own sense of purpose in this world. Research on resilience to severe stress concludes that a key element in recovery is the cultivation of a sense of personal meaning. Even when everything seems to be going well, a life without personal meaning may seem empty and pointless.

SURVIVAL OR RESILIENCE: THE ROAD TO PERSONAL MEANING

Overcoming stressful obstacles is an essential part of healthy identity development. From childhood and adolescence to early adulthood through the end of life, you are confronted with many real-life obstacles in becoming yourself and attaining your goals. But it is your own attitude that can be the greatest obstacle of all. Thirty years of social research and recent neuroscience reveal that one of the core ingredients in the formula for resilience to chronic or severe stress is the cultivation of personal meaning derived through reflection about your stressors. Holocaust survivors, Vietnam prisoners of war, hurricane and earthquake victims, or people who grew up with abuse or chronic social stressors are at high risk for long-term emotional and physical damage. Surviving these acute or chronic stressors often means years of pain and suffering, but resilience to them is a result of five key ingredients:

1. Extinguishing the physiological stress triggers
2. Psychological reframing of the experience
3. Developing coping skills

4. Establishing healthy emotional bonds
5. Developing personal meaning in your life to protect you from stress.

My own experience with a conflict between my true wishes and my fears of displeasing my father during my medical school training makes this point.

TO BE OR NOT TO BE: ARTIST OR DOCTOR?

I had always felt that my own true identity was that of an artist. But as I grew up, I remember my father, a dentist, lamenting that he had not gone to medical school and become a doctor. To be true to myself and to please my father, I came up with a solution: I would attend medical school *and* continue making art. When a classmate asked me what I intended to specialize in, I answered, "Psychiatry—it seems to be the most conducive to my artistic temperament." My classmate was dumbfounded: "So psychiatry is for doctors who don't want to be doctors!" he told me.

His statement rang true. I realized there and then I did not really want to be a doctor. My poor academic performance showed the lack of passion I had for my studies. Then, when I failed pathology and had to repeat the year, I felt utterly humiliated. I went into a career crisis. Should I drop out and go to art school? Or should I take the year over again?

My dad drove down to Galveston from Port Arthur to help me sort out my dilemma. While we walked on the beach, I confessed I had never really wanted to be a doctor—I had only gone to medical school to please him. My dad was surprised, but he made it absolutely clear that he only wanted me to find my true path. "If you want to go to art school, son, I'll support you." Feeling a newfound sense of freedom, I chose to continue with medical school anyway. My rationale was simple: as a psychiatrist I can be my own patron. I can pursue my art career on the weekends. But I cannot be a weekend doctor if I am an artist.

Over the course of my career, I have come to love the art of medicine by integrating my true self with the demands of making a living. I have transformed my life by discovering an authentic sense as a creative physician. One of my mentors in medical school, William Bean, director of the medical humanities department, encouraged me to write since I was so full of questions about meaning, culture, and art. Recent developments in neuroscience allow me to integrate both art and science into a creative life of writing that will, I hope, connect with many more people than I could see in my office. What greater gift of meaning could I give myself in my career? I have been forever grateful to my dad for that conversation. He helped liberate me from my greatest phantom stressor.

Question 3: What Am I Doing Here? Resilience for New, Secure Attachments

Buddha said that suffering is rooted in the attachments we make during the course of our lives. An updated developmental neuroscience version of Buddha's profound observation may go something like this: *The secure attachments in life that are necessary for healthy development can be vulnerable to stress. When insecure attachments emerge from early life stresses, they can negatively affect us throughout our lives.* Recent studies of adverse childhood experiences dramatically support the wisdom of the Buddha.

New studies point to the cause of addiction being rooted in early-life stress, not exposure to addictive substances or drug dealers. Additionally, these studies show a direct correlation between overall health status and adverse childhood experiences. The conclusion made by this research is that the enemy to our physical, emotional, and mental health depends largely on how we treat each other, especially during the early years of life. These findings make a strong case for doing everything you can to liberate yourself from the long reach of phantom stress. By using your reflective powers to explore your adverse childhood experiences, you take a step toward transforming these destructive, nonconscious emotional memories into harmless memories of emotion.

The short answer to 'What am I doing here?' is found implicitly in George Santayana's famous quotation at the beginning of this chapter: *"Those who cannot remember the past are condemned to repeat it."*

IMPERFECT MEMORY: THE LONG SHADOW OF ADVERSE CHILDHOOD EXPERIENCE

Who would you be without your memories? When we tell our stories to others, we toggle back and forth in time, relying on our memory to reconstruct a particular experience. But memory is not perfect. It is merely a reconstruction by our brain that is often different from the experience as it actually happened. Sometimes details are lost, but the gist is there. At other times, we just cannot come up with what we are looking for, though we know we once had the information. Memory's imperfection can protect you from remembering traumatic events. Or it can haunt you for a lifetime.

Most people believe that memories are immutable, but there are many different ways to impair recollection. Memory is not like a movie that can be played over and over again, always remaining exactly the same. Memory is subject to change. Each time a memory is called to mind and then placed back into storage, it becomes vulnerable to alteration.

Why can you not recall being a baby even when you look at images or listen to sounds from your infant years? This is because the hippocampus, the part of the brain that stores retrievable memories of early experiences, does not begin to function until you are about three years old. Memories stored before the age of three are exclusively emotional memories mediated through the nonconscious brain circuits of the amygdala. Nonetheless, when something in the present triggers a nonconscious, emotional memory, your brain and body simulate many of those same early physical conditions: the fear, racing heart, and sweaty palms. You have just been visited by phantom stress. You may not even be aware of what triggered you, but your body remembers. You simulate those early physical conditions in the present to inform you of what you felt back then—fight or flee. With phantom stress your body tells you that you have received the message, "Danger!" but you have misread its source. The danger is not in the room, it is in your head.

You know that phantom stressors are the nonconscious emotional memories of adverse events from childhood that activate emotions and allostatic changes in the body state in the present. In step 1, you learned to decline the invitation that phantom stress triggers. In step 2, you learned to refocus your attention and recover adaptive conversations. Now it is time to use your reflective powers to liberate yourself from the grip of phantom stress. By reflectively exploring adverse childhood experiences in your own quiet time, you will be able gradually to transform these emotional memories into harmless memories of emotion.

TOM AND MEREDITH: "GHOSTS IN THE NURSERY"

Meredith and Tom did Logosoma Brain Training early on in their relationship. After they identified their core issues with insecure attachment and neutralized many of their phantom stress triggers, they needed very few coaching sessions. They had become a skilled team. But their lives changed dramatically when their son, Andrew, was born.

The younger of two brothers, Tom always felt he had been seen as second best in his parents' eyes. Nothing he did seemed to compare with his brother Peter. Peter appeared to have a monopoly on their mother's attention. Tom also felt that Peter was the favorite son of their lawyer father. Peter wanted to study law and be "just like dad." At home, Tom took on the demeanor of a chronic sad-sack, full of despair and hopelessness. But when the boys went out to play with neighbors, it was Tom's genuine charm that found validation with his peer group, not Peter's. Tom's social skills were his strength. When Tom and Meredith met in high school, it was the charm she fell for, believing she was the luckiest girl in town.

When Tom and Meredith became parents, the harmony that they had achieved through Logosoma Brain Training needed maintenance. Shortly after their son Andrew was born, Tom felt the loss of Meredith's radiant attention. As Meredith focused so intensely on baby Andrew, Tom went spiraling into his own phantom hell, feeling and acting like a sad-sack all over again. He was reliving the time when he felt his mother chose Peter over him. Tom was in the grip of his phantom stressors.

Poor Meredith, clueless as to what was happening to her husband, was also sucked into her own phantom nightmare. Her father had been a brooder. He would sit in front of the TV every night, silently drifting into his own world. Occasionally, he would explode. Meredith's mother was terrified of her husband's episodic rage attacks. They created a chronic state of high anxiety for herself and her children. So when Meredith looked at Tom's frozen face, it triggered the memory of her raging father, causing her to freeze up herself.

By reflecting, Tom began to see how his fear and despair were inappropriate. When he asked himself, "What am I afraid of?" he was able to unveil the source of his phantom stressors. "'I guess I'm not afraid of anything here and now. As a child, I was afraid that my mother didn't love me. Meredith's attention and love for our baby triggered one of my phantom stressors. And I didn't even know how! I'm actually overjoyed about having a son. And I'm delighted to see that Meredith is a wonderful mother. We are all very happy."

When Tom asked himself, "What do I want?" he was able to discover his wishes. His realization, "I want to be the best husband and dad I can be," clearly liberated him from his phantom fears. In his newfound freedom, Tom recovered the joy and focus on his wife and son. Needless to say, as Tom and Meredith worked together, each reflecting on their phantom stressors from childhood, they were able to neutralize the ghosts in the nursery and make lasting changes in their attitudes and behaviors. By reflecting, Tom was able gradually to live out his wishes, rather than being a hostage to his fears. As he reframed his experience from the insecure past to the strong, warm bonds with Meredith and Andrew, saying no to the past made his life improve in the present. With Tom's ghost in the nursery vanquished, Meredith found herself liberated as well. The grip that phantom stress had had on the new family was displaced by joy and a deep, secure attachment between them all.

MEMORIES, DREAMS AND REFLECTIONS: A PERSONAL INVENTORY

Any therapist can tell you that making a personal inventory of your history of successes and failures can stir up significant emotional memories, both positive and negative. By going to therapy and discussing these issues over time, you can discover patterns of emotion, thought, and behavior that developed from adverse childhood experiences in your attachments. By reflecting on your memories and dreams, you can create new solutions for old problems that will rewire your brain patterns for healthier adaptive attitudes and behaviors.

You can also accomplish many of the same goals with reflection. But you must be willing to commit to the effort. By examining and accepting your past, by cultivating an attitude of gratitude for your brain's neuroplasticity, and by embracing the responsibility for your future, you are three steps closer to vanquishing the power that phantom stress exerts on your life.

Be patient. Reflecting on your memories and rewiring your brain takes months of repetition. If you find this step too scary or too painful to do alone, then you would probably do well to seek professional guidance. Therapists provide more or less objective observations for your life story. They can help you reflect on your emotional memories so you can start to reframe the real story of your past and neutralize the negative emotional memories.

Brain Scan: Transforming Emotional Memories into Memories of Emotion

Emotional memories can intrude into consciousness with powerful physiological symptoms. When this happens, you have an opportunity to transform these toxic, frightening images into less potent memories of emotion. So what makes this possible?

Today, scientists believe that memories are rewritten every time they are recalled in a process called reconsolidation. Instead of recalling a fixed memory that has been created months, years, or even days ago, the brain retrieves the memory and then modifies it with here-and-now beliefs and experiences. This gives the old memory an entirely new context. It becomes slightly altered. So what does this mean for you? When you remember and reload an event in your brain, you are essentially creating a new memory. The old memory is actually shaped by the changes that have occurred in your brain since it was last recalled.

Simply put, the reconsolidation model of memory explains that every time you remember something, it gets reloaded in a different form. That is the beauty of neuroplasticity. The more you reflect on your past and modify your memories with current grounded assessments, the less they will be able to trigger a stress response.

I invite you to begin practicing reflection by focusing on your emotional memories. Reflecting is an exercise that you can do almost anywhere. And all it costs is the time it takes to do it.

Integrating Reflection and Meditation

Modern reflective techniques developed by psychotherapy and ancient meditation training are skills that can be learned. Both will enhance your brain's built-in ability for reflection. In the reflecting processes, you revisit your negative emotional memories to reconsolidate them into harmless memories of emotion, helping you become your authentic self. Meditation uses your reflective skills to observe the spontaneous workings of your mind. You become the spectator of your thoughts and emotions without getting engaged with them. By becoming an observer of your emotional and mental processes, you start to develop a new awareness of your mental activity. As you cultivate the ability to watch the antics of your mind, you will gradually be able to start letting go of your attachment to the drama your mind spontaneously creates. One benefit of this letting go practice is to increase the time between your impulse to act and the execution of that action, increasing the time available to exercise *free won't*. Cultivating the gap between impulse and action is one of the key skills involved in your ability to regulate your emotions. By doing so, you will gradually master the stress response triggered by threatening memories, images, thoughts, or feelings. Research on meditators has shown that the practice of meditation over time increases attentiveness, enhancing the ability to make accurate assessments.

What is the difference between reflection and meditation? When you are reflecting on the three questions, *Who am I? What does it all mean? What am I doing here?* you are uncovering emotional memories about of yourself that may be hidden from consciousness. Your attention becomes engaged, forming an attachment to the thoughts and feelings on which you are reflecting. You start to identify the unconscious puzzle fragments of your phantom stressors by bringing them into consciousness so you can reflect on what they mean.

When you meditate, your conscious attention is simply watching the spontaneous flow of your mind. You remain detached from the conscious flow of thoughts and feelings, unlike reflection when your attention is searching to make meaningful connections between past events and present emotions. With meditation, you observe and feel all of your mental activity without engaging with it. Relaxing your body by concentrating on your breathing will help you better resist the temptation to pursue your thoughts and feelings. Your mission is to observe the activity of your awareness only, without engagement or attachment. Just watch the parade of thoughts and feelings across the screen of consciousness.

Meditation also kindles memory, especially the previously unconscious emotional memories we know as phantom stressors. As they emerge, your stressors will certainly trigger your amygdala. But instead of continuing to engage with your stressors, you will take the high road to your PFC and simply observe your stressors now. You watch as the emotions flow through your body, even feeling your heart rate increase and then subside, without ever becoming attached. When the phantom stressor and its subsequent emotional charge pass, a new implicit memory is created. Meditation offers a powerful tool to help your brain rewire itself, especially when it comes to taming the amygdala's triggering of phantom stress. Meditation is the observation of mental and emotional activity from a point of stillness. Watch your thoughts. Watch your emotions. Be still.

Exploring your negative emotions with reflection in a mental state of meditative relaxation enhances self-awareness and neutralizes toxic memories. Observing your inner mental life by meditating allows your attention to regulate negative emotion and deepens your acceptance of your own humanity. This experience—of feeling intense negative emotion without acting out a stress response—kindles compassion for yourself and others when you recall how destructive one can become based on intense, irrational fears.

Watching your own mind can be fun, serious fun. Be still. Do not follow, do not explore, *just pay attention!*

Chapter 8

STEP 4: RECONNECT WITH THE POWER OF WE

> *The love you take is equal to the love you make.*
> —**Beatles**

Over the course of this book, we have seen how stress, in all its insidious forms, can take your brain hostage by triggering you to relive stressful memories from the past, disconnecting you from the present. The final step in Logosoma Brain Training is nothing short of a new beginning for all your relationships. You will learn to *reconnect* with your body, yourself, those you love, your work, and your environment. This step empowers you to strengthen and deepen your emotional networks with others in a new and far more intimate way. By reconnecting with the power of We, whether you are single or in a relationship, you will tap into an inexhaustible source of resilience and creativity, the wellspring for personal meaning. When you have become mindfully aware of just how you have suffered from the emotional disconnection caused by phantom stress, the isolation and loneliness of being stuck in the past, you can truly appreciate the power of your connections in the present. Cultivating an attitude of gratitude will facilitate reconnecting with all of your relationships.

WHAT IS RECONNECTING?

Your brain is wired to connect. From the molecular level of neurotransmitters to the complex interactions between neural networks, it is designed to create connections. Neuroscience has discovered that even our most routine encounters act as regulators of how our brain orchestrates our emotions. The more strongly you connect with someone, the greater the benefits. Our ability to connect starts during infancy. Infant researchers have discovered that well-adjusted mother-infant interactions go through a pattern of connection-disconnection-reconnection that unfolds over a few minutes. The connection phase is marked by joint attention and reciprocal positive emotion. If, however, either the baby or mother disappoints the other, the connection is interrupted. This disconnection is stressful and triggers negative emotions. For example, a mother holds a baby in her lap. They are playing with a squishy toy, each taking turns in delighting the other. But when the baby diverts his attention away from the toy and gives a good hard tug on mother's hair, she winces in pain. Although the mother's angry grimace lasts only a microsecond, as she says "Ouch!" and pulls her head away from the baby, he is startled by the sudden change in his mother's facial and behavioral cues. The baby begins to cry, appearing quite confused. When the mother realizes that her reaction has frightened her baby, she focuses her attention to soothe the situation. She uses a calming voice and attentive empathetic facial gestures that say "I'm sorry." A successful reconnection between mother and her baby renews the smiles and laughs of the happy pair. Secure mother-infant attachments emerge from thousands of repetitions of this cycle during the early years of development. The roots of a true self have their beginnings in this foundation of interpersonal connectedness.

Secure adult emotional relationships share these same patterns of connection-disconnection-reconnection, but they are far more complex than the infant-mother story. In fact, when adult connections get derailed and are not followed up with efforts to reconnect, they often develop into chronically stressed relationships. The reconnect step is your guide to regaining joint attention. After successfully *refusing* the stress trigger, you are able to start *refocusing* your attention to moderate the effects of stress hormones. By *reflecting* on your phantom stressors, you can start to *reconnect* with other brains. Reconnecting is a two-way street, a reciprocal activity that involves all of your senses, your thoughts, your feelings, and your memories. Reconnecting with your relationships provides an ongoing opportunity to explore the very essence of your being and share this meaning with the people you want to connect with.

Brain Scan: Oxytocin, the Calm and Connect System

In order to survive, you need to be able to fight and flee from danger. But in order to thrive, we need to relax, to bond, and to heal. You have a built-in hormonal system that is involved with relaxation and bonding. This calm and connect system (CCS) is mediated by the hormone oxytocin, the polar opposite of the stress hormone adrenaline which triggers the fight/flight reaction systems in the body.

The CCS slows down your heart rate and stimulates your digestive system. During rest, this system is busy helping your body grow and heal, changing nourishment into energy and storing it for later use. A single injection of oxytocin in rats triggers higher blood pressure and elevates stress hormones. But repeated injections bring on the calm and connect effect characterized by lower blood pressure and reduced muscle tension. The CCS stimulates social contact between individuals and promotes mating behaviour. It increases maternal behaviour, even in females that have never had pups. An abundance of oxytocin diminishes pain sensation and causes wounds to heal faster. Studies show the CCS facilitates learning in rats, even when they have learning disabilities. The CCS effect puts the mind and body in an optimal state for reflection, creativity, learning, and problem solving. As oxytocin helps you recover from stress, the focus of your attention shifts from fear-driven vigilance to curiosity and a wish to explore the environment. You feel friendly rather than distrustful. In this physiology of peace and tranquillity, you can lower your defenses. You can shift your attention to others. You become open, sensitive, and emotionally ready to explore connecting with others.

Oxytocin is produced by both males and females. It can easily be released in both sexes through pleasant warmth, hugs, cuddles, rhythmic touching, and massage. Oxytocin appears to be the hormone of *skinship*, the positive physical experience of connecting with others. Skinship and emotional bonding are the two body guardians of Logosoma Brain Training. By integrating them with positive memories and your story of We, you lay the foundation for life-long secure emotional attachment. Nature has clearly designed reciprocal physical stimulation in partnerships to kindle long-term intimacy. From the intensity of making love, to the soothing touch of massage, to the reassurance of a hand on the shoulder or the trust in holding hands, human touch kindles connectedness immediately. Human touch in a trusting relationship has been shown to lower blood pressure. The same touch can trigger a stress response when the context is inappropriate or unsafe. A lack of physical contact will actually increase your vulnerability to the ravages of the stress hormones adrenaline and cortisol. Perhaps the most extreme example of this is the now famous discovery of what is called *failure to thrive*, a syndrome identified in post-World War II orphanages by Rene Spitz. Babies in these orphanages were hygienically cared for and well nourished, but failed to grow. They eventually died in high numbers. The cause was discovered to be the lack of physical contact. No one was picking up the babies and cuddling them. Oxytocin drives maternal and nursing behaviour which in turn triggers the impulse of feeding and growth in the infant.

Scientific research has proven that emotional bonding in all your connections—from your mother-infant attachment to your adult relationships—provides powerful protection from chronic stress. Oxytocin plays a critical role in the balancing of the calm-and-connect system and the fight/flight/freeze system, creating a dynamic interplay for survival, growth, and adaptation. Together, they cover all the necessary ingredients for our resilience to stress, helping us to form secure bonds and perpetuate our species.

Armed with this new understanding of the power of your connectedness to others, your efforts to create deep and lasting connections with your partner, your family, and your friends will be well worth the time and emotion you invest.

THREE PHASES OF RECONNECTING

As we have seen, connecting and reconnecting is a complex molecular-sociological cycle that occurs over the course of your entire lifetime. Logosoma Brain Training focuses on three essential phases:

1. *Irresistible invitations,* which help you recover the lost joint attention with others so you can reconnect
2. *Relationship maintenance conversations,* which are preventative dialogues to help you cope with life's natural bumps that can cause disconnections in your relationships
3. *Serious fun,* which is the creative and exploratory joy resulting from successful reconnections

The Rose Family: A Saga of Reconnections

For more than twenty-five years I have consulted with many families spanning four generations. To give you a summary of how critical reconnecting is for resilience in all your relationships, I have created the Rose family saga, a story that covers many years. The saga is a consolidation of many case studies from my private practice into a single, multigenerational family. I hope the story illuminates how reconnecting facilitates healthy development, recovery from stress, and creative adaptation to the suffering that life offers.

Here is the cast:

Bob: Successful director of a family business
Alison: Retired teacher, socially active in charities
Ted: First born, works in advertising, married to Nancy, prekindergarten teacher; together they have one child, Timmy, aged six
Sara: Second born, lawyer, single but in long-term relationship with Mark, an actor, a law school classmate of Sara who dropped out to pursue his passion to act

You will follow Bob Rose and his family over a 20-year period through their Logosoma Brain Training to illustrate three phases of reconnecting.

First Contact: Bob and Alison say, "Our teenage son, Ted, is a monster!"

This is Bob and Alison's Frankenteen story of Ted's teenage years of drugs and sociopathy.

My first contact with the Rose family was to evaluate Ted, Bob and Alison's teenaged son, for substance abuse and oppositional behaviors. Ted was on the brink of getting kicked out of his private school for smoking pot on campus. "I've been caught stealing money from my mother. Dad's loaded but he never gives me a cent unless I listen to his humiliating lectures about how hard he had it as a kid. He's such a control freak, constantly bossing everyone about. I feel like I'm walking on eggshells all the time. I never know when dad's going to start screaming at me, telling me I'm a failure. I'm so stressed out that

I've started scratching my arms with a pin to calm myself down," Ted reported.

Bob Rose was enraged at his wife and son. "Ted never eats with us anymore, so we never know what he's doing at night in his room. One evening, I went upstairs to find out. I knocked on the door but he didn't answer. So I just went in. I found Ted passed out on the floor lying in his own urine. I was terrified and called an ambulance. We rushed him to the emergency room. His blood tests showed he'd taken an overdose of heroin, for God's sake! Alison always makes excuses for Ted, no matter how serious the problem is. She's spoiling that kid. She caught him stealing money from her purse the other day and did nothing! Listen, I had plenty of stress when I grew up but I didn't resort to stealing from my parents and taking drugs! I'm ready to kick them both out!" Bob complained.

It was clear that Alison enabled and minimized Ted's problems. Bob's constant threats to call the police to deal with Ted or to divorce Alison made things even worse. The level of daily tension at the Rose family home was so high that they were all paralyzed by fear; hostages of chronic stress. Ted's way of dealing with the stress by self-mutilating himself was my first concern. He needed professional help. So we decided to send him away for a year-long residential treatment for multiple drug addiction. Then Bob and Alison began their Logosoma Brain Training with a focus on parenting.

PHASE 1: THE IRRESISTIBLE INVITATION

How Logosoma Brain Training helped Bob and Alison learn to reframe their feelings of being hostages to Ted's behaviors and reconnect with their son to help him recover from addiction.

What do family members want more than anything from each other? Almost every teenager who I have consulted with over twenty years has stated without coaxing, "My parent's don't listen to me; they don't care what I think." We all need to be listened to, genuinely given serious attention. It feels great when we get it. We all need attention and validation. Validation secures connectedness and intimacy through positive physical, emotional, conversational, and remembered experiences.

Talking about emotional issues with his son was extremely uncomfortable for Bob. His father was never emotionally open or available, so he had no model. But Bob was a perfectionist so he took his Logosoma Brain Training seriously. When he realized it was much like going to the gym with a personal trainer, he became a dedicated practitioner.

I coached Bob by saying, "To make an irresistible invitation authentic, you must focus your attention on the right target. If you're speaking authentically from your true self, expressing your genuine wishes to reconnect, the message will penetrate your son's defensiveness. What you don't want to do is trigger Ted's defenses and fears. You don't want to mobilize the phantom stressors imprinted in his memory circuits by your past critical behaviors toward him. Remember, you're inviting Ted into an exploratory dialogue, not an interrogation."

Bob got the message. He began using our training sessions to help him find his true voice, so that he could convey his genuine wish to connect with his son.

Ted returned home monthly on weekends for family meetings. Many parents find it difficult to voice their emotions to their teenage children. Bob's training helped him face his own troubled teen years. By confronting his fears and reflecting, Bob began to realize that he always yearned to be emotionally closer to his own father. This awareness helped him approach the challenge with his son. With the aid of the sample scripts below, Bob was able to offer an irresistible invitation for emotionally reconnecting with Ted that was authentic, loving, and compassionate.

SAMPLE SCRIPT 1

"Son, I've recently realized just how little I really know about you. I want to know more. My work with the doctor has really helped me to reflect about life—your life, my life and our life together—in a new way. I feel kind of lonely doing this by myself though. I hope you'll join me from now on. I know we haven't had many discussions about your dreams, what you want, what you hope for, and what you'd like to be doing in the future. I want to change this. I'd love to hear about your own thoughts and feelings from now on so I can better understand you—and us!"

SAMPLE SCRIPT 2

"I've recently started reflecting on issues I've always run away from. And I discovered that I haven't been a very good listener. I've never really listened to anyone, especially you. I've never heard about your dreams and wishes, or how you see yourself. And honestly, I'd love to know more about who you are. Sometimes, I sit across the room from you and think, 'I love my son. I want him to enjoy our life together. I want to stop my busy day and give him my full attention—to really listen to what he has to say.'"

Bob began to realize that his estrangement from his own father as a teenager was repeating itself with Ted. But Bob had a choice. He could choose to be a different kind of father. After a year of monthly meetings, Bob and Ted finally bridged the gap between them. Their reconnection provided the secure attachment Ted needed to help him through recovery from addiction to heroin.

ALISON TO SARA: "MARK IS NOT FOR US!"

When Sara falls in love with Mark, she and her mother, Alison, encounter a normal developmental bump in their relationship. Can they work it out?

During our first session, Sara, aged twenty-five, started complaining about her mother, Alison. "She's threatened to disinherit me if I stay with Mark. I met him during law school. Mom adored the idea I'd marry a lawyer. Dad has more than a hundred lawyers working under him, so he was indifferent. Mark dropped out of law school in his second year. He decided to pursue his lifelong passion, acting. I was so proud of him! When I shared my feelings with my mother, she reacted with the sharpness of a guillotine: 'Drop the dropout. He's not for us!'"

Soon afterward, Sara came in for a session with both her parents. The session was little more than a display of Alison's stonewalling, a sign of serious dysfunction in families characterized by emotionally shutting others out by closing down. "I'm not here to listen," said a defiant Alison "I want to be heard. I will not come to another session with Dr. Romero until Sara gives up on Mark. I will not support my daughter's misguided love affair," Alison declared.

Bob was virtually silent during the entire session, despite being coaxed to speak by all parties. His eye contact and body language with Sara spoke volumes. Seated between Sara and Alison, he leaned toward his daughter and hardly looked at his wife during the entire consultation. When Alison's posture stiffened as she gave her final decree, Sara slumped, weeping into her hands. Bob reached out and held his daughter's hand. His eyes misted as he attempted to hold back the emotion.

I knew the chance of reconnection between Sara and her mother was very remote for the moment. After validating Alison's opinion and showing empathy for her plight, I told her that I would always be open to listen to her or help the situation in any way. Alison deflected my best effort to maintain a therapeutic alliance with her by repeating, "If you get her to drop that boy, I'll be happy to come in again. I hope I've made myself perfectly clear!" With that, she raised herself from the chair and walked out the door, as if for the last time. But I knew it was not Alison's last visit.

Sara came back with Mark for Logosoma Brain Training and Bob paid for it. The young couple came seeking help to navigate the stress put on their own relationship caused by Alison's attitude toward Mark.

Sara and Mark: To Be or Not to Be . . . We

How Sara and Mark learned to reconnect as a We team despite the efforts by Alison to destroy their connection.

By the time Sara and Mark came in for a consultation as a couple, they were nearly ready to split. "Why would I want to marry into a family with a mother-in-law who publicly despises me?" Mark lamented. "I understand," said Sara despondently. "I'm not worth the stress. I'm sure you can do better. After all, she's my problem, not yours."

As their Logosoma Brain Training progressed, the couple discovered they were being held hostage by a stress reaction caused by a hostile force. Its name was Alison—the "mother-in-law!"

Sara and Mark learned to *refuse* Alison's stress invitation. They learned to *refocus* their joint attention on their hope and dreams of a happy life together. After considerable personal *reflection*, they began courageously to liberate themselves from Alison's invitation to suffer. Although they failed to *reconnect* with Alison, they were able to declare their love, take ownership of themselves as adults, and accept a chronically stressful disconnection with Alison. In following their authentic wishes, Sara and Mark reconnected, forming a powerful and resilient alliance, the narrative of We.

Bob's implicit validation of Sara's wishes gave her strength to stand up to her mother's domination. Bob never actually defied Alison, but by

PHANTOM STRESS

not condoning her rejection of Mark, Bob's behavior communicated his support for his daughter Sara.

When I asked Sara what she thought her father would say about her relationship with Mark she answered, "I think dad would tell me to follow my heart. I feel that he's always supported me, especially when mom goes over the top with her need to meddle. I feel that dad really loves me for who I am, not who I like. I trust his love much more than I trust my mom's, even though I know she only wants the best for me. I don't think she can really accept me for who I am—but dad does."

BOB AND ALISON: TO SPLIT OR TO RECONNECT?

In the aftermath of Alison's battle with Sara over Mark, Alison felt betrayed by Bob for not supporting her in her condemnation of Sara. Bob had his first emotional meltdown when Alison threatens divorce. Bob called for emergency couples Logosoma Brain Training to save their marriage.

Late one evening, the phone rang. It was Bob—and he was frantic. "Sorry to call so late, Doc, but I've got a real problem. Alison's moved out. She's gone to our apartment in Boston and won't take my calls. I'm going crazy. I need your help," Holding back the tears, he takes a deep breath and continues. "It has been three days since she last spoke to me. I've never seen her like this. She's so angry. I'm afraid she might do something crazy. You gotta help me, Doc, please help me!" he pleaded.

After calming him down, Bob began to reflect over the next few days. He had never felt so helpless in all his life. "I've always been in control of the situation whether I'm at work or with my family. But I don't know how to deal with this kind of craziness," he confided.

Acting as a mediator, I contacted Alison and brought her together with Bob for their first effort to focus their joint attention on their own relationship.

HE SAID; SHE SAID

Bob and Alison mirror each other with negative assessments.

Sitting in my office, facing each other like adversaries, the war of the Roses began. Bob took the first shot in the form of a negative assessment. "Doc, she's like a German general. She never stops telling me how much better I can do. Enough is enough! I think I've done a

153

great job providing a secure life for everyone. The family business is triple the size of what it was when we inherited it. My family should be very grateful."

Alison was having none of it. She returned Bob's negative assessments with a few of her own. "Doctor Romero, Bob has a fax machine in the bedroom! He's actually answered his cell phone when we were having sex! Believe me; I've tried to be a good wife. I've always supported him in everything he does, even when it fails. He lost millions in that desalting seawater venture but I never said a word. He eats butter like I eat yogurt. He's going to kill himself with all the stress he brings on. When he wouldn't back me up on the Mark issue it was the last straw. I had to leave."

ALISON AND BOB: "I CHOOSE YOU AGAIN!"

Alison and Bob demonstrate how LBT helped them learn to reframe their hostage relationship into a We team.

Before Alison and Bob started Logosoma Brain Training they were at a crossroads in their relationship. Would it be lawyers or brain training? By following the training, they chose not to talk to lawyers. They chose each other. When they each uttered "I choose you again," Bob and Alison embarked on a journey to create a new intimacy in their relationship. They were ready to grow beyond a game of swapping criticisms and one-upmanship. Instead, they chose an experience of communion between their essences.

Second time around, Alison and Bob were in the process of falling in love by design—not by hormonally driven urges or physical attributes (she's beautiful and subservient; he's handsome and rich). As a couple, they were in a proactive position, an extremely creative position in the life story of We. They were building a solid sense of their identities. They were coming to accept life on life's terms, remembering to find gratitude for everything that was going well instead of focusing on what was not. Knowing that crises will occur, Alison and Bob nonetheless refused to accept that invitation to worry about tomorrow. Instead, they helped each other focus intensely on the present problems until they found a solution—together.

Like Alison and Bob, you can practice new attitudes and behaviors as a team. It will strengthen both of you and secure your relationship as a sanctuary from stress. To ensure you continue to practice your

Logosoma Brain Training together, I have developed a protocol for We team communication. I call it a relationship maintenance conversation.

PHASE 2: RELATIONSHIP MAINTENANCE CONVERSATIONS—THE WE TEAM

The purpose of a relationship maintenance conversation (RMC) is to provide your We team with some practice in joint attention and reciprocal communication over difficult issues, ones that undermine trust and respect in human relationships. The primary goal of the RMC is *better listening*. Consider this the war room for strategic planning against the stresses of everyday life and phantom stress. Remember, stress, not your partner, is your enemy. The format used (see below) is a guide for turn-taking conversations. By using a turn-taking structure for these meetings, you agree beforehand to inhibit your urge to interrupt the speaker. Focus on listening to your partner, not to your reactions to their comments. Let your partner finish what he or she is saying. In my professional practice, I train couples and families to take turns talking about fears, concerns, and requests.

Take Bob and Alison as an example. If Bob reports two fears about himself, one fear about Alison and one fear about them as a couple, I instruct Alison to listen silently until Bob is finished. Taking notes often helps the listener to focus. Then I ask Alison to respond with her feelings, observations, and questions. Bob must listen until she is finished. The meeting concludes when both of their issues have been discussed to their mutual satisfaction, or until they agree to continue the meeting at another time.

Take a look at the chart below. Each set of boxes (fears, concerns, requests) is considered one conversation topic. A ten—to twenty-minute time limit is recommended for each set of boxes.

His	Hers
Fears What feelings of fear do you have about **yourself** in this partnership? What feelings of fear do you have about **your partner**? What feelings of fear do you have about **your partnership**?	**Fears** What feelings of fear do you have about **yourself** in this partnership? What feelings of fear do you have about **your partner**? What feelings of fear do you have about **your partnership**?
Concerns What observations concern you about **yourself** with regard to your partnership? What observations concern you about your **partner**? What observations concern you about your **partnership**?	**Concerns** What observations concern you about **yourself** with regard to your partnership? What observations concern you about your **partner**? What observations concern you about your **partnership**?
Requests What requests would you like to make to your partner about **herself**? What requests would you like to make to your partner about the **partnership**?	**Requests** What requests would you like to make to your partner about **himself**? What requests would you like to make to your partner about the **partnership**?

In the beginning, when there are many issues to address, I recommend weekly, half-hour RMCs. You can take longer with complex issues if you need to, but do not go beyond an hour. Remember, the primary goal is to *reconnect*. Solving the issue is not the primary goal, it is simply the payoff. The goal is to reconnect through better listening. Your stress levels will naturally subside. The RMC helps you establish the new way to react to old problems by reconnecting through establishing joint attention.

A word of caution: If one of you is triggered during the RMC, then stop! Remember the drill. Refuse the stress conversation and take a break. Then you can reschedule a new time to resume.

BOB AND TED: PHANTOMS IN THE BOARDROOM

Bob gets taken hostage by phantom stress; Ted nearly relapses into addiction.

When Bob announced his plans to retire, Ted returned home to stake his claim to run the family business. As Bob never talked about the family's business affairs with Ted, Ted's return home took Bob by surprise. Bob returned to my office shortly after Ted arrived. "I'm both elated and terrified by Ted's sudden wish to join the family business. I have no idea what kind of businessman he will be. Sure, my lifelong dream was to grow the business and pass it on to my children. I trust Sara's legal education and her solid character. But I'm still haunted by Ted's reckless impulsivity during his teen years."

Bob did not realize that his real problem was not his concern about Ted's past. Ted already had twenty years of recovery under his belt. After his recovery, he had become a successful advertising executive with a keen sense for marketing. Ted had his own lifelong dream of taking over the helm of the family business someday. He wanted to prove to his father that his reckless teenage years were long past. Bob's phantom stressors, his nonconscious fears, derailed any rational thinking about Ted's readiness to take over. Ted's return triggered Bob's long forgotten battle with his father, Milton.

Milton had had a serious stroke when Bob was 19, forcing Bob to take a leadership role in the business at a very young age. "Dad could hardly speak," Bob recalled, "But the little he managed to say made it clear he did not approve of my taking over our operations. Nonetheless, I dropped out of college to come home and help my father. Two years later he was dead and I took over. I had good advisors. And mother was very reassuring. But something was missing. I never got dad's blessing.

It's haunted me till this very day. I've tried hard to do what I thought would please him."

Bob had never discussed the struggle with his father with anyone. Emotionally, he felt like he was right back in the thick of that tragic, terrifying two-year hell. His judgment was clouded by Ted's addiction, so he attacked him with one criticism after another.

When Ted came to see me, he confessed, "I've come closer than I have in twenty years to start using drugs again. My dad is so totally unreasonable and closed-minded about me. I've been completely professional in presenting my credentials to dad and to the board of directors. I brought letters of recommendation from my firm and top clients. The board unanimously endorses my taking the job! I just don't understand why my father is still against me. Perhaps I should just give up."

THE ULTIMATE LESSON: BOB DISCOVERS THE MEANING OF IMPERMANENCE AND FINDS GRATITUDE

In the escalating stress over Ted's bid for leadership, Bob has a myocardial infarction, a heart attack. Bob mobilizes an emergency effort to control everything.

When Bob stopped listening to me and everyone around him, his relentless, self-induced stress triggered a serious heart attack, leaving him too weak to function. Nonetheless, he still struggled to control his doctors, his treatment, his family, and his business from his hospital bed during his recovery.

"I'm feeling so helpless," Bob moaned. "I've never felt like this before. I'm afraid to die, Doc. I need your help. I feel like everything I've done in my life is coming back to haunt me. I can't sleep. And when I do, I have nightmares about how ruthlessly I've acted. I see all the people I've fired or the companies that I've taken over only to dismantle—it's horrible! And I keep seeing my dad too, just standing at the foot of my bed scowling at me, like he's waiting for me to die!"

Bob's guilty nightmares were sending him into a condition of such severe chronic stress that it could have been fatal. I urged him to practice his focusing techniques and to meditate so his body could relax. "Just watch your thoughts and feelings," I coached him during a meditation session at his bedside. "If it's time for you to leave your body, then let it go with gratitude and respect. You can finally surrender your need to control everything. Let it go!"

A few weeks later, I arrived at the hospital for another bedside session to find a transformed man. Bob had emotionally surrendered his effort to control his life. "I finally understand what you mean by *acceptance*, Doc. Life is constantly changing. Nothing lasts forever, no matter how much I try to control it. I can finally see that I've never really controlled anything. I've just tried to. And I've nearly killed myself in the process! I feel that I've hurt so many people, especially my own family."

Bob's confrontation with his own mortality kindled a radical transformation. By having the time to reflect, he was awakening to a deep, personal, understanding of his own impermanence. "I finally know why you are always urging me to accept life and to be grateful for life as it is," he said smiling. "I'm so grateful for my family. They've been so wonderful. And Ted has been the best. He comes every day and has been so loving. I can't believe how I've abused him for so many years."

BOB SURRENDERS AND FINDS AUTHENTIC JOY

Facing his own death, Bob surrenders his lifelong obsession with control.

"I don't know how long I have to live," Bob reflected while still in the hospital. "But I know that I want to change my life. I'm ready to take instructions, Doc. I want to learn how to change my attitude. I want this feeling of peace to last. It's a deep calm, like I've never felt before. Even if I die now, it's OK. Ha! Who would have guessed that Bob Rose would ever find peace in giving up control! I'm a very pragmatic man, Doc. I've never been religious or even remotely interested in anything spiritual. It always seemed so flakey. But after facing death myself, something spiritual awakened in me. Please help me learn how to hold on to this feeling of gratitude and acceptance for life, Doc. I want to feel like this forever!"

Bob's thoughts of the past were suppressed, and his mind was not burdened with plans for the future. He found liberation from all of his obsessive schemes for control by refocusing on the present moment. All sense of emotional urgency vanished. Bob's ensuing sense of release was felt as a deep calm. His body recovered from fight/flight stress hormones and increased production of oxytocin, the calm/connect system. And something totally unexpected occurred: Bob had what many call a spiritual awakening. At long last, Bob's mind experienced a sense of liberation from all his expectations and fears. So what exactly happened to Bob's brain to cause this?

BRAIN SCAN: THE GOD MODULE

Imagine you are part of an experiment. You are in a neuroscience lab comfortably seated in an overstuffed chair. EEG connections are placed on your head to record your brain waves. A helmet designed to gently pulse weak magnetic fields into your brain is fitted onto your head. Then you are blindfolded and instructed to report your feelings. The experiment begins with transcranial magnetic stimulation of your brain in varying areas. The neuroscientist stimulates the right temporal lobe. A mild surge in electrical activity, called a temporal transient, emerges and you exclaim, "I suddenly feel a great sense of comfort and safety. I feel the presence of someone here, someone who is going to take care of me. If I die, I'm not afraid." You have just experienced the triggering of the *god module*, the neural network that, when activated, provides a conscious sensation of peace and tranquility in the face of mortal danger.

One hypothesis is that this sensed presence is the prototype of the *God experience*, the perception of being connected to an all powerful, benevolent other. It is similar to what is observed during studies of the brains of long-term meditators. The meditators report feeling "connected to the universe," or feeling "a deep sense of peace" when at the peak of a meditation session. Scientists believe these temporal transients are the biology behind the experience of prayer, religious conversion, and even the spiritual awakening reported during times of crisis and grief. They also believe that, to one degree or another, they occur in all of us.

So what is the evolutionary purpose of a god module? For the adults like Bob, the god module may kick in when one is faced with overwhelming fear or life-threatening experience. The circuits automatically trigger a soothing experience to the terrified adult producing a calm, clear brain, able to reflect in a time of crisis, unafraid of any threat. The paralyzing anxiety is tranquilized by the perception of a benign presence that will comfort you, even in the face of death. This may be an evolutionary feature in our brain, nature's built-in remedy for the existential anxiety that emerged when humans first became consciously aware of the sense of self.

WHAT? ME WORRY? BOB BEGINS THE RECONNECTION PROCESS

Bob survived his heart attack and underwent bypass surgery. Forced to slow down during recovery, he began a process of transformation. He restarted his Logosoma Brain Training with a new vigor and focused on reconnecting with himself and all of his botched relationships.

"I'm beginning to realize that what I was chasing for most of my life was approval from my father," Bob reflected. "Worrying all those years got me here!" Bob's sense of humor and joking about himself was a healthy sign that his fears were starting to dissipate. "For me, happiness meant that dad would be happy with my performance in life. I'm beginning to see now that if I want true happiness, I have to change my way of interpreting the world. I have to learn the new skills of acceptance and gratitude in every thing I do, great or small. I'm starting to surrender my obsession with controlling everything since I finally see I can't really change other people or control what happens in the world. What's so invigorating is the knowledge that I can change myself! I can learn new ways to look at my life and my family. I'm feeling a deep sense of peace and joy in just being present. In being reconnected with my family, I feel like I'm living in a miracle, a new life," Bob reported in a calm voice.

Bob was now ready for the final phase of reconnection training, serious fun.

PHASE 3: SERIOUS FUN

I developed the term *serious fun* after watching three-year-olds during interactive play. At two years old, toddlers can only do parallel play. They treat each other more like objects than another baby, acting emotionally aloof. When one takes a toy from the other, causing it to cry, there is a complete disregard for the other's crying. By three years old, children graduate into reciprocal play. This is a social affair, a turn-taking drama with joint attention to a single focus, like stacking blocks together or rolling a ball back and forth. When children are at play, their attention is intensely focused. Their mood is joyful. They are creating serious fun! Even when disruptions in play occur and feelings are hurt, toddlers will tend to soothe each other. They make the effort to reconnect for more shared fun. You can see serious fun as early as the first weeks of life between the beaming face of a new mother and her smiling infant. Focused connections that kindle joy and happiness form the essence of serious fun.

Serious fun is rooted in the child's positive emotions coupled with exploratory and experimental interaction with others and the environment. These positive experiences facilitate creative problem solving and experimenting. The soothing effects of serious fun enhance brain development in children with secure attachment and encourage resilience in children with insecure attachment. These serious fun experiences during early development lay the foundation for optimal adaptive resilience for the individual. When serious fun is a shared experience, it connects us with each other. I believe the experience of serious fun is at the emotional core of creativity and experimentation in the arts and sciences in all cultures. When we bring focused attention into our adult social connections, our careers, and our intimate relationships, we open ourselves up to better connectedness.

BOB LEARNS TO CREATE SERIOUS FUN

Reconnecting with his own childhood wishes, Bob opens a gateway to his nonconscious emotions and embarks on his own path toward personal redemption

Practicing the art of relating to other people without being controlling challenged Bob in every way: cognitively, emotionally, and motivationally. It took a near-death experience to awaken Bob to the preciousness of each moment and to motivate him to change his obsession with control. He was finally willing to take responsibility for a fundamental shift in his attitude toward looking at himself and his perception of the people, places, and things around him. Accepting the truth of his own powerlessness to change others made Bob finally realize he can only change himself.

In reconnecting with his own wishes, Bob reawakened a lifelong secret desire, to return to playing the piano. He had taken lessons as a child and loved it. But he dropped playing when Milton told him that teenagers who were not going to become professional musicians should put away the toys of childhood and get serious about school. Bob's cardiologist was overjoyed with the idea—as long as he did it for pleasure, not competition.

In the months after his bypass surgery, Bob hired a teacher and began learning to play a favorite, Beethoven's *Für Elise*. Bob told me, "Taking lessons has really helped me learn to surrender to someone else. I was the one who had to follow the orders. And then one day, in the middle of a lesson, I suddenly burst out in tears. I thought I was losing it. I got so emotional!"

In our work together, Bob remembered that he had played this piece at a third grade recital. Milton had come to watch, a rare experience for little Bob. He recalled that his father was proud of his performance, one of the few validating memories that he had with Milton. "I was totally unaware why that piece was the first thing I wanted to relearn," Bob said. "But after that flood of tears, I felt that my proud dad was right next to me, smiling."

MUSIC, EMOTION, AND THE BRAIN

In the last ten years, a pioneering group of neuroscientists, psychologists, and musicians have been exploring the relationship between music and the brain.

As a music lover, I was curious to find out what the study of music might offer my patients in terms of emotional regulation and stress reduction. I attended three conferences on the neurosciences and music. My reaction to these conferences helped me explore my patient's music history. Based on the compelling evidence from the neuroscience of music, we see the close neural links between music and emotion. Similarly, researchers have identified close neural links between language and stress.

I am convinced that music is an important vehicle for sharing emotional experience and connecting with each other. I also believe that music can be used to facilitate *reconnecting*. Music dissolves the social boundaries and cultural customs that distance us. It holds the power to unify and synchronize the brains of people from disparate beliefs.

Most would agree that music has a direct impact on our emotional state. For example, most people can tell when a piece of music makes them feel angry or happy. Certain musical emotions, like facial expressions such as sadness, anger, and fear, are almost universally recognized. The happy and sad emotional tones tend to be among the easiest ones to communicate in music. Like facial expressions, these emotions might be expressed by similar structural features across musical styles and cultures.

Music expresses emotion. It is a medium for passionate communication. With or without musical training, your brain is a natural-born musician. Spoken language communicates ideas. The emotional message packed into spoken language is called prosody, the music of language. The term refers to the emphasis or inflection placed on words and phrases. It is interesting that women are more sensitive to prosodic cues than men. People with musical training are better able to distinguish prosodic elements than those with an untrained ear. By practicing his piano, Bob learned to become more sensitive to his emotions and the emotional cues in others.

Numerous studies have demonstrated the beneficial effects of listening to music in reducing stress in a variety of challenging situations, including artificially induced stress in laboratory rats, preoperative, and procedural stress during colonoscopy, and presurgical stress in children. Further studies in corporate employees show recreational music-making, such as group drumming, enhances mood states and regulates natural killer cells. Music-making has also been shown to lower the levels of gene expression for cytokines, the process by which a gene's DNA sequence is converted into the functional proteins of the cell. Remember, cytokines are protein by-products of the immune system, triggered by the stress response, which can wreak havoc on your immune system, your energy level, your mood, your sleep cycle, your appetite, and even your clear thinking.

The mounting research in neuroscience and music validates the wise proverb, *music soothes the savage beast*. It echoes my own experience that Chopin and Debussy are the perfect antidotes for a stressful day at the office.

AFTER HIS DANCE WITH DEATH, BOB LEARNS TO DANCE FOR LIFE

Bob accepts Alison's lifelong wish to take dancing lessons. Up until now, Bob "never had time."

When Bob was cleared by his cardiologist to take dancing lessons, he and Alison began weekly sessions. During one romantic lesson, Bob proposed to Alison again. "I told her that the doctor had prescribed that I get creative and have some serious fun in my relationships. Marrying

Alison was one of the happiest days of my life. So I said 'let's get married again and invite all of our family.' Alison practically flipped with joy!"

Reconnecting to his life with a newly cultivated attitude of acceptance and gratitude for life as it is made Bob's creative circuits hum. He planned a surprise for Ted at the wedding reception. Bob decided to announce his retirement as CEO of the family company and honor the board's wishes to install Ted. Only Bob and the board members knew, so when the reception happened, there was more than one reason to celebrate a new chapter in the Rose family saga.

In the months that followed, Bob saw me less frequently. "You're navigating life in a new identity," I explained to him. "You've discovered generosity and compassion. And for the first time in your life, you can openly discuss your emotions. The hard work you put into your Logosoma training has rewired your brain circuits for optimal adaptive resilience. You're on your way to exploring life in fresh ways."

Bob smiled and shared his latest round of serious fun with me. "Ted and I have set up a foundation for charitable giving. Sara is going to oversee it for the moment, but we want all of the family to participate. I finally realize that a life of accumulating wealth can be toxic unless you recycle your gains!"

Once we both felt that Bob no longer needed to see me regularly, we left it as a "call me if you need me" relationship. In saying farewell, I offered Bob one of my favorite quotations:

> *Old men ought to be explorers*
> *Here and now does not matter*
> *We must be still and still moving*
> *Into another intensity*
> *For a further union, a deeper communion*
> *Through the dark, cold and empty desolation,*
> *The wave cry, the wind cry, the vast waters*
> *Of the petrel and the porpoise. In my end is my beginning.*
>
> T. S. Eliot, Four Quartets

REFLECTIONS ON CONNECTEDNESS

Neuroscience has ushered in a new age in understanding *what* we are, *how* we come to be ourselves, and *where* this new paradigm of humanness can take us in the future. I believe that the molecular basis of human connectedness invites a renewed faith in our deep ability to care about ourselves, each other, and the environment in which we all must live. The critical importance of connectedness at every level of existence, from the molecular world of DNA to the socio-cultural world of our everyday lives guides my practice as a psychiatrist. Being connected to my body, myself, my family, my friends, my colleagues, and my world, enriches my life as a person. I hope that Logosoma Brain Training inspires you to *refuse* the invitations to stress, *refocus* your attention for resilience, *reflect* on the meaning of your life, and *reconnect* with all that you love.

Glossary

adrenaline (epinephrine). A 'fight or flight' hormone that is released from the adrenal glands whenever danger threatens. When secreted, it floods out from the endocrine gland into the bloodstream to prepare the body for action in emergency situations. The hormone boosts the supply of oxygen and energy-giving glucose to the muscles, making the individual more mentally alert and physically strong; it also ensures that only vital bodily processes occur. Epinephrine plays a central role in the short-term stress reaction—the physiological response to threatening, exciting, or environmental stressors such as high noise levels or bright light.

allostasis. A swift and intricately organized physiological response to help keep the body stable (*homeostasis*). It is mediated by a system for communication that links the brain, the endocrine system, and the immune system.

allostatic load. The result of chronic activation of the stress response system that impairs the allostatic system from properly shutting down. Neuroscientist Bruce McEwen describes it as "the wear and tear that results from chronic overactivity or underactivity of allostatic systems."

allostatic system. An integrated communication system comprised of the nervous system, endocrine system, and immune system that controls heartbeat, blood pressure, and similar functions to keep the body stable (*homeostasis*) especially during a stress response.

amygdala. The almond-shaped amygdala is located in the brain's medial temporal lobe. It forms part of the limbic system and is believed to play a key role in emotional learning. It is comprised of many nuclei with more than 700 interconnections throughout the brain, and is reciprocally connected with the hypothalamus, the hippocampus, and the thalamus. In humans and other animals, it coordinates autonomic and endocrine responses in conjunction with emotional states, and it is linked to both fear and pleasure responses. Its size is positively correlated with aggressive behavior across species. In humans, it is the most sexually dimorphic brain structure, and shrinks by more than 30 percent in males upon castration. Conditions such as anxiety, autism, depression, narcolepsy, post traumatic stress disorder, phobias, and schizophrenia are suspected of being linked to abnormal functioning of the amygdala.

anterior cingulate cortex. A specialization of the neocortex with functions central to intelligent behavior, such as emotional self-control, focused problem solving, error recognition, and adaptive responses to changing conditions.

autopoeisis. A theory of life that was developed by Chilean scientists Humberto Maturana and Francisco Varela. The theory proposes that "living beings are characterized in that, literally, they are continually self-producing . . . They differ from each other in their structure, but they are alike in their organization (in that they are autonomous). A system is autonomous if it can specify its own laws, what is proper to it."

body maps. Neural mappings of the body state located in various parts of the cortex and limbic brain that are believed to give rise to conscious awareness of feelings. Antonio Damasio notes, "The hypothesis that when feelings occur there is a significant engagement of the areas of the brain that receive signals from varied parts of the body and, as a result, map the ongoing state of the organism. Those brain areas, which are placed at several levels of the central nervous system, include the cingulate cortex; two of the somatosensory cortices (known as the insula and SII); the hypothalamus; and several nuclei in the brain stem tegmentum (the back part of the brain stem)."

bottom-up message. Neuroscientist Michael Posner defines bottom-up messages as "those processes that are driven automatically or reflexively by stimulation even when the person is instructed to be passive toward the event." For example, the amygdala receives a stress message directly from the body that triggers a stress response. Neuroscientist Joe LeDoux calls this scary route to the amygdala "down and dirty," or "the low road," characterized by the fact that you jump before you think.

Brain generation. Refers to the emergence of the new neuroscience in the last fifteen years and our increasing interest in the workings of the brain that underlie all that we do as human beings, including our cultural activities.

cognitive. Having a basis in or reducible to empirical factual knowledge; the mental process of knowing, thinking, learning, and judging.

cortisol. The stress hormone produced in the adrenal cortex that mediates allostasis. It belongs to a class of hormones called glucocorticoids. When it becomes elevated during chronic stress, it can cause significant damage, even cell death, to the hippocampus, and many other tissues in the brain and body.

cytokines. Protein molecules produced by activated immune cells which play an important role as bidirectional mediators between the immune and nervous systems. Stress induces cytokine gene expression and evokes the release of cytokines and the hormone, corticotrophin-releasing factor, the trigger for cortisol production. Dysfunctional effects in this system include sleep disturbances, appetite, mood, cognition, sex drive, energy, and fatigue levels. Cytokines have been implicated a wide variety of mental and physical disorders including but not limited to depression, anxiety, chronic pain, immune disorders, and chronic fatigue.

down-regulate. A cool-down period of allostasis, mediated by the hippocampus, that occurs after a stress response. Its purpose is to lower stress hormones to recover homeostasis and to avoid escalating the stress situation.

emotional memory. A kind of implicit memory formed during a highly stressful event that impairs the ability to retrieve it as a memory. It may be encoded in fragments or as features of the context in which the danger occurred, and it can be activated outside of awareness. Once activated, the same physiological intensity is mobilized as if the event were happening again. This is the cause of flashbacks in posttraumatic stress disorder. High levels of cortisol during the original stressful event impair the hippocampus's ability to form a clear explicit memory, but those levels of cortisol do enhance the amygdala's ability to form an implicit memory of the danger. Phantom stress results from emotional memories. (Compare with *memory of emotion,* below.)

ethology. The scientific study of comparative animal behavior founded by Konrad Lorenz.

explicit memory. Memories formed by conscious learning and consolidated through the hippocampus for long-term storage in the cortex. These memories are retrievable by conscious effort and are also referred to as declarative memory. Examples include reading and writing.

false self. A term coined by psychoanalyst D.W. Winnicott to indicate the organization of an infant's sense of self. That self is essentially compliant (false) to a mother who fails to meet the infant's spontaneous self-expressive gestures with validation; instead she substitutes her own gestures. Winnicott describes this failed mothering as the "not good enough mother." In adult relationships, the false self shows up as people-pleasing behaviors, white lies, and other behaviors beyond ordinary social politeness. When the false self governs one's relationships, it is to the detriment of one's true self, and self-sabotaging attitudes of resentment and self-pity prevail, as well as self-sabotaging behaviors.

fMRI (functional magnetic resonance imaging). fMRI is a technique for determining which parts of the brain are activated by different types of physical sensation or activity, such as sight, sound, or the movement of a subject's fingers. This brain mapping is achieved by setting up an advanced MRI scanner to track the increased blood flow to the activated areas of the brain.

gene expression (or simply **expression**). The process by which a gene's DNA sequence is converted into the functional proteins of the cell. Nonprotein coding genes (e.g., rRNA genes, tRNA genes) are not translated into protein.

Gene expression is a multistep process that begins with transcription of DNA into messenger RNA (mRNA). Transcription is followed by posttranscriptional modification of the amount and timing of appearance of the functional product of a gene. After this, mRNA leaves the cell nucleus. mRNA is then translated by the ribosome to produce a polypeptide. Further changes may then occur through posttranslational modification.

Any step of gene expression may be modulated, from the transcription step to the posttranslational modification of a protein. Gene regulation gives the cell control over structure and function, and is the basis for cellular differentiation, morphogenesis and the versatility and adaptability of any organism.

good enough mother. (Winnicott) The mother who facilitates the development of her baby's true self by meeting his or her core needs.

hippocampus. A part of the brain located inside the temporal lobe (humans have two hippocampi, one in each side of the brain). It is part of the limbic system and plays a role in memory, emotional regulation, and navigation. The name derives from its curved shape, which is said to resemble a seahorse. It plays a central role in the formation of new memories and the retrieval of memories.

hypothalamus. A region of the brain located below the thalamus, which forms the major portion of the ventral region of the diencephalon. It functions to regulate certain metabolic processes and other autonomic activities. The hypothalamus links the nervous system to the endocrine system by synthesizing and secreting neurohormones often called *releasing hormones.* These hormones function by stimulating the secretion of certain hormones from the anterior pituitary gland—among them, gonadotropin-releasing hormone (GnRH). The neurons that secrete GnRH are linked to the limbic system, which is highly involved in the control of emotions and sexual activity. The hypothalamus is also the area of the brain that controls body temperature, hunger and thirst, and circadian cycles.

implicit memory. Memory characterized by a lack of conscious awareness of the act of recollection, or unconscious recollection of prior experience; also referred to as nondeclarative or procedural memory. For example, when you ride a bicycle, you are unconsciously remembering the necessary skills.

learned helplessness. A term created by psychology research scientist Martin Seligman to designate a condition that results from chronic stress and leads an animal or human being to give up on life, even when escape is possible.

molecular sociology. (B. McEwen) The study of the molecular and cellular mechanisms in animals and humans regarding the impact of stress on the brain resulting from the effects of social interactions.

memory consolidation. The process by which recent memories are crystallized into long-term memory. Consolidation is used to refer to two distinct processes:

The molecular process by which long-term conductivity of synapses is affected. Memory consolidation occurs after training or a single exposition of a cell to a stimulus-response pair. When weak and strong inputs to a cell are active at the same time, the weak pathway is strengthened by way of its association with the strong pathway. This is called Hebbian plasticity, after the psychologist Donald Hebb, and is a model for how learning occurs in the brain.

The movement of episodic memory into the neocortex. Many researchers believe that episodic memories are initially stored in the hippocampus and are slowly moved (consolidated) into the neocortex. This process of consolidation may happen during sleep, perhaps during dreaming.

There is evidence that recall puts memories into an unstable, labile state, and that after recall, the memory must be reconsolidated or it will be forgotten. Memory reconsolidation occurs during the review or repetition of the learned material. Maximum consolidation with minimum time investment is achieved by means of closely spaced repetition.

memory of emotions. Emotional experiences, positive and negative, enhance the hippocampus's ability to encode explicit memories. Emotional experiences from the past are more easily retrieved when the present mood is similar to the remembered emotion (happy or sad times are more easily recalled if you are feeling happy or sad). The intensity of the original physiology is not reactivated by the retrieval of these memories of emotion unless a link with the amygdala has been reactivated. (Compare with *emotional memory*, above.)

mirror neurons. Neurons that fire both when performing an action and when observing the same action performed by another person. As a result, the neuron "mirrors" the behavior of another neuron as though the observer were performing the action. Mirror neurons appear to be critical in understanding action and imitation, which are important in social, emotional, and language learning. These neurons were discovered in primates (by Giacomo Rizzolatti), and have been observed in some birds, and in humans in the speech area (by Pierre Paul Broca) and the inferior parietal cortex of the brain. Some scientists (V.S. Ramachandran, for one) consider mirror neurons to be one of the most important findings of neuroscience in the last decade.

negative assessment. A criticism or an attack on your behavior, your language, or any part of yourself.

neural architecture. Networks of neurons with synaptic interconnections that form functional networks, such as the frontal attentional network of mirror neuron system.

neuron. The impulse-conducting cells of our brains, which are comprised of a cell body, a long arm called an axon, which extends to another neuron, and the dendrite at the end of the axon, which stores the neurotransmitters for release into the synaptic space for neural transmission; also called nerve cell.

neuroplasticity. Refers to the brain's ability to remodel itself by physically changing in response to stimulus and activity. It is strongly believed to be the physical mechanism of learning. The neurophysiologist Donald Hebb developed the theory of neuroplasticity.

neurotransmitter. A chemical substance, such as acetylcholine or dopamine, that transmits nerve impulses across a synapse, the space between the dendrite of one neuron and the cell body of another.

OCD (obsessive-compulsive disorder). An anxiety disorder characterized by recurrent thoughts, impulses, or images that a person recognizes to be a product of his own mind (obsession), as well as repetitive behaviors (compulsions, for example, hand washing, checking, counting, praying) that the person feels driven to perform in response to the obsession. This disorder has been shown by psychiatrist Jeffrey Schwartz to involve a malfunction in a feedback loop between the frontal cortex and the limbic brain.

olfactory. Relating to, or contributing to, the sense of smell.

optimal adaptive resilience. The best possible response of an individual, couple, or group to adverse circumstances. An individual's level of resilience depends on a balance of biology and individual differences in temperament, ability to cope with stress, and early childhood experiences. Features of resilient behavior include psychological reframing of the stressful experience, reflective ability to create positive personal meaning from the stressful experience and ongoing skill to navigate current difficulties.

orbitofrontal cortex (OFC). A piece of prefrontal cortex that sits just behind the orbits of the eyes and performs some of the most advanced functions of the brain. The OFC is an association area, coordinating signals and relaying disparate types of information. The OFC is privy to a wealth of information from sensory, emotional, and memory-related brain regions and thus serves as an important center for integration and evaluation. It is believed to be a major site, or at the very least an essential participant in a network of sites, where sensory and memory-related information is transformed into decisions and actions.

oxytocin. A short polypeptide hormone that is released from the posterior lobe of the pituitary gland and stimulates the contraction of the smooth muscle of the uterus during labor. It also facilitates release of milk from the breast during nursing. This hormone provokes the calm and connection response to stress, and is more prominent in females, although it is also found in males. Its production can be increased by warm, soothing touch.

pain. A survival alarm experienced as an acute, episodic, or chronic unpleasant sensation occurring in varying degrees of severity as a consequence of tissue damage, separation and loss, and shame.

PET scan (positron emission tomography). A computer-generated image of biological activity within the body that is produced through the detection of gamma rays that are emitted from positrons. Positrons are ephemeral subatomic particles emitted from radioisotopes of carbon, nitrogen, oxygen and fluorine.

PFC (prefrontal cortex). The prefrontal cortex is the anterior part of the frontal lobes of the brain, lying in front of the motor and associative areas. Divided into the dorsolateral, orbitofrontal, and mesial prefrontal areas, this brain region has been implicated in planning complex cognitive behaviors, personality expression, and moderating social behavior. The main activity of this brain region is considered to be the orchestration of thoughts and actions in accordance with internal goals.

posttraumatic stress disorder. A psychiatric disorder that can occur following a traumatic event in which the person experienced or witnessed an event that involved actual or threatened death or serious injury, or a threat to the physical integrity of self or others, and in which the person's response included intense fear, helplessness, or horror. In children, the disorder may be expressed by disorganized or agitated behavior. The traumatic event is persistently re-experienced in one or more of the following ways: recurrent and intrusive distressing recollections of the event, recurrent distressing dreams of the event, acting or feeling as if the traumatic event were recurring (sense of reliving the event, hallucinations, illusions, dissociative flashback episodes), intense psychological distress or physiological reactivity at exposure to internal or external cues that symbolize or resemble an aspect of the traumatic event. Persistent avoidance of stimuli associated with the trauma and numbing of general responsiveness as indicated by efforts to avoid thoughts, feelings, conversations, activities, places, or people associated with the event. The disturbance causes significant distress in social, occupational, or other important areas of functioning or impairs the individual's ability to gain help for the disorder. Depending on the resilience of the individual, the condition can resolve itself without treatment or can become chronic and debilitating.

resilience. The complex interactive process of risk and protection that involves both genetic and environmental influences in the adaptation to and recovery from adversity.

somatosensory cortex. This is a prominent structure in the parietal lobe, behind the central gyrus, and is the location of the primary somatosensory cortex, the main receptive area for the sense of touch.

stonewalling. A term coined by marital researcher John Gottman, which refers to an extreme form of obstructive and defiant behavior that hinder interpersonal communication.

synapse. A specialized junction through which cells of the nervous system signal to one another, as well as to nonneuronal cells such as muscles or glands, through neurotransmitters. A synapse between a motor neuron and a muscle cell is called a neuromuscular junction.

top-down message. Neuroscientists Posner and Raichle define top-down messages as those that "are generated by the person internally, usually with his active attention." This definition indicates that voluntary attention (through the prefrontal cortex) drives the message.

true self. (Winnicott) A true self develops when the "good enough mother" supplies sense to her baby's actions, and provides the beginning life story for the baby's body.

Logosoma Terminology

adaptive conversation. A conversation that navigates the stress triggers and maintains the elements of trust and respect. It includes two people with a single goal. As a shared narrative experience, it depends on joint attention to the emotional changes within each partner.

hostage relationship. A condition in which a marriage or partnership is locked in a destructive pattern of behavior and communication that results from chronic stress. It is characterized by compulsive negative assessments, breakdowns in reciprocal listening, inability to sustain joint attention, poor emotional regulation, and simultaneous feelings of resentment and self-pity in the partners.

CI (connectedness inventory). A document that asks questions to reveal levels of connectedness in relationships. It consists of statements about your views and experience of your partner's attitudes and behavior regarding physical intimacy (skinship), emotional bonding, language, and environment.

life story. Human beings are a *body* living in a *life story.* Our life stories are ever changing and consist of our thoughts, opinions, beliefs, memories, and emotions.

limbic script. Narratives, both conscious and unconscious, that are laid down early in life and are charged with emotion and unconsciously influence action in the present. These scripts may be positively charged (for example, being inspired by a parent or teacher to pursue a career) or negatively charged (for example, being abused by a parent, which creates a script that children are uncontrollable, which leads to the abuse of one's own children).

Little me. Your little me, often referred to as the *inner child*, is a sense of yourself housed in the emotional memories from your past. Your little me never grows up. In fact, little me is like a phantom stressor in that anything in the present that reminds your little me of a past emotional experience, positive or negative, can trigger childlike feelings.

Logosoma Brain Training. A mind-body training program developed by Phillip Romero, MD, based on current models of neuroplasticity and ancient mindfulness meditation. Through the use of conscious, focused attention, reflection, and remembering of painful past events, the training empowers one to neutralize the negative effects of stress, particularly phantom stress, and to create a resilient and adaptive true self, a competent and creative attitude toward partnerships, and a sanctuary of trust in intimate attachments.

mindful awareness. Mindful awareness integrates both Eastern and Western reflective tools, meditation and psychotherapy. Mindful awareness empowers the brain to learn new ways to solve old problems. Using mindful awareness, you can learn to observe your mind without stress and liberate yourself from the hostage-like feelings and physiology produced by chronic stress. Mindful awareness is a practice of effortful attention, which has been shown with brain imaging technology to enhance positive emotion and improve focused attention.

partnership maintenance conversation. A formally scheduled, turn-taking, partnership exercise designed to enhance joint attention and emotional regulation through the use of implicit and explicit memory.

phantom stress. A stress response triggered in the present by a benign stimulus that is unconsciously linked to an emotional memory. The emotions and physiological intensity from the past are reawakened by a stimulus in the present triggering an allostatic reaction. Like a phantom limb, these negative emotions from the past can cause pain and inappropriate destructive behavior in the present.

sanctuary of We. A safe haven from uncertainty where one experiences a sense of comfort and control—a place of welcoming and nurture that meets your needs. It derives from human attachment between true selves, and is the adult equivalent of the infant's holding environment with the "good enough mother."

serious fun. Rooted in childhood play, serious fun entails the simultaneous experience of high level focused attention with emotions of joy, excitement, and spontaneous creativity. When serious fun is activated during reciprocal play, partners enjoy a deep sense of connection and well being that enhances their "We" narrative with positive, long-term memories.

stress conversation. A conversation with oneself or with another person that triggers the allostatic response and leads to a cascade of defensive and retaliatory thoughts or behaviors. In turn, those thoughts and behaviors often become self-sabotaging and destructive to the bond of trust and respect in a partnership.

stress trigger. A feeling that something is not right. A stress trigger causes adrenaline to flow into your blood, reaching your brain and triggering the survival response to freeze, flee or fight. This brain trigger leads to 'butterfly stomach,' sweaty palms, an uneasy quiver in the knees, poor concentration, and fear of the unknown.

suffering. An irrational fear of pain in the future that triggers the body in the present to fight, flee, or freeze.

Bibliography

Aggleton, J. *The Amygdala.* Oxford: Oxford University Press, 2000.

Arbib, M. *Action to Language via the Mirror Neuron System.* Cambridge: University Press, 2006.

Austen, J. *Zen and the Brain.* Cambridge, MA: MIT Press, 2000.

Austen, J. *Zen Brain reflections.* Cambridge, MA: MIT Press, 2006.

Avanzini, G., et al. *The Neurosciences and Music.* New York: Annals of the New York Academy of Sciences, 2003.

Avanzini, G., et al. *The Neurosciences and Music II,* New York: Annals of the new York Academy of Sciences, 2005.

Avanzini, G. et al. *Neuromusic News, neuromusic@fondazione-mariani. org,* 2007.

Baron-Cohen, S. *The Essential Difference: The Truth About the Male and Female Brain.* Perseus, 2003.

Begley, S. *Train Your Mind, Change Your Brain.* New York: Random House, 2007.

Benson, H. *The Relaxation Response.* New York: Harper, 1975.

Benson, H. The Harvard Guide to Lowering Blood Pressure: Boston, 2006.

Bertalanffy, L. von. *General System Theory.* New York: George Braziller, 1968.

Bowlby, J. *Attachment and Loss.* New York: Basic Books, 1969.

Bowlby, J. *A Secure Base.* New York: Basic Books, 1988.

Cacioppo, J. T. et al. *Foundations of Social Neuroscience.* Cambridge, MA: MIT Press, 2002.

Campbell, J. *Pathways to Bliss.* Novato, California: New World Library, 2004.

Charney, D., et al. *Neurobiology of Mental Illness.* New York: Oxford University Press, 1999.

Chess, S. & Thomas, A. *Temperament: Theory and Practice*. New York: Bruner Mazel, 1996.

Coates, S., et al. *September 11: Trauma and Human Bonds*. New York: Analytic Press, 2003.

Cozolino, L. *The Neurosciecne of Human Relationships*. New York, Norton, 2006.

Crick, F. *The Astonishing Hypothesis*. New York: Touchstone Books, 1995.

Cross, I. *Neurosciences and Music*. New York: Annals of the New York Academy of Sciences, 2003.

Damasio, A.R. *The Feeling of What Happens*. New York, Harcourt, Brace, 1999.

Damasio, A. R. *Looking for Spinoza*. New York, Harcourt, 2003.

Darwin, C. 1872, *The Expression of the Emotions in Man and Animals*. London: Oxford, 1998

Davidson, R.J. *Handbook of Affective Sciences*. New York: Oxford, 2003.

Edelman, G. and G.Tononi. *A Universe of Consciousness*. New York: Basic Books, 2000.

Ekman, P. *What the Face Reveals*. New York: Oxford University Press, 1997.

Ekman, P., et al. *Emotions Inside and Out*. New York: Annals of the New York Academy of Sciences, 2003.

Frankl, V.E. *The Will to Meaning: Foundations of and Applications of Logotherapy,* New York: Penguin, 1969.

Fisher, H. *Why We Love*. New York: Henry Holt, 2004.

Gazzaniga, M.S. *The Mind's Past*. Los Angeles, University of California Press, 1998.

Goleman, D. *Emotional Intelligence*. New York: Bantam, 1997.

Goleman, D., and Dalai Lama. *Destructive Emotions*. New York: Random House, 2003.

Goleman, D. *Social Intelligence*. New York: Random House, 2006.

Gopnik, A. et al. *The Scientist in the Crib*. New York: Morrow, 1999.

Gottman, J. *The Seven Principles for Making Marriage Work*. New York: Crown, 1999.

Gottman, J. *The Mathematics of Marriage*. Cambridge, MA: MIT Press, 2002.

Harlow, H. *From Learning to Love*. New York: Praeger, 1986.

James, W. 1890, *The Principles of Psychology.* New York: Henry Holt, 1950.

Joseph, R. *Neurotheology.* San Jose, CA: University Press, 2003.

Juslin and Sloboda. *Music and Emotion.* Oxford: Oxford University Press, 2002.

Kandel, E. R. et al. *Principles of Neuroscience.* New York: McGraw-Hill, 2000.

Kielcolt-Glaser, J. et al. *The Physiology of Marriage* New York: Elsevier, 2003.

Koch, C. *The Quest for Consciousness.* Colorado: Roberts and Company, 2004.

Lane, R. et al. *Cognitive Neuroscience of Emotion.* New York: Oxford University Press, 2000.

LeDoux, J. *The Emotional Brain.* New York: Simon & Shuster, 1995.

LeDoux, J. *The Synaptic Self.* New York: Viking, 2002.

Ledoux, J., et al. *The Self from Soul to Brain.* New York: New York Academy of Sciences., 2003.

Levenson, R. *Blood Sweat and Fears: The Autonomic Architecture of Emotion in Emotions Inside and Out.* New York: New York Academy of Sciences, 2003.

Lorenz, K. *The Natural Science of the Human Species.* Cambridge, MA: MIT Press, 1996.

MacLean, P. *The Triune Brain.* New York: Plenum Press, 1989.

Maturana, H., and F. Varela. *The Tree of Knowledge.* Boston: New Science Library, 1987.

McCrae, R.R. *Handbook of Personality.* New York: Guilford Press, 1999.

McEwen, B.S. *The Hostage Brain.* New York: Rockefeller University Press, 1994.

McEwen, B.S. *The End of Stress As We Know It.* Washington, D. C.: Joseph Henry Press, 2004.

McEwen, B.S. et al. *The Unity of Knowledge.* New York: Annals of the New York Academy of Sciences, 2001.

McEwen, B.S. et al. *Resilience in Children:* New York: Annals of the New York Academy of Sciences, 2006

Moberg, K. *The Oxytocin Factor.* Cambridge, MA: Da Capo Press, 2003.

Newburg, A., et al. *Why God Won't Go Away.* New York: Random House, 2001.

Nisbett, R. 2003. *The Geography of Thought.* New York: The Free Press, 2003.

O'Connor, R. *Undoing Perpetual Stress.* New York: Penguin, 2005.

Panksepp, J. *Affective Neuroscience.* New York: Oxford University Press, 1998.

Pederson, B.K. et al. *Cytokines in Aging and Exercise.* Int. J. Sports Medicine: May, 2000.

Peretz, I. in Juslin & Sloboda ed. *Music and Emotion:* Oxford: Oxford University Press, 2002.

Peretz, I. & Sloboda, J. *Neurosciences and Music II:* New York: Annals of the New York Academy of Sciences, 2005.

Persinger, M. in Joseph, R. ed. Neurotheology. University Press, 2003.

Piaget, J. *The Psychology of the Child.* New York: Basic Books, 1969.

Plotnikoff, N., et al. *Cytokines: Stress and Immunity.* Boca Raton: CRC Press, 2007.

Posner, M. et al. *Cognitive Neuroscience of Attention.* New York: Guilford, 2004.

Posner, M., and M. Raichle. *Images of Mind.* New York: Scientific American Library, 1994.

Ramachandran, V. S. *Phantoms in the Brain.* New York: Morrow, 1998.

Rees, E. *September 11: Trauma and Human Bonds.* New Jersey: Analytic Press., 2003.

Reisberg, D. et al. *Memory and Emotion.* New York: Oxford University Press, 2004.

Tronick, E. *The Neurobehavioral and Social Emotional Development of Infants and Children.* New York: Norton, 2007.

Sapolsky, R. M. *Why Zebras Don't Get Ulcers.* New York: Freeman, 1999.

Schacter, D. L. *The Seven Sins of Memory.* Boston: Houghton Mifflin, 2001.

Schore, A. Affect Regulation and the Origin of the Self. New Jersey: Lawrence Erlbaum Associates, 1994.

Schore, A. Affect Regulation and the Repair of the Self. New York: Norton, 2003.

Schwartz, J. *Brain Lock.* New York: Regan Books, 1996.

Schwartz, J. *The Mind and the Brain.* New York: Harper Collins, 2002.

Seligman, M. *Authentic Happiness.* New York: Simon and Shuster, 2002.

Selye, H. *The Stress of Life.* New York: McGraw-Hill, 1956.

Sternberg, E.M. *The Balance Within.* New York: Freeman, 2001.

Theorell, T. *Everyday Biological Stress Mechanisms.* Basel, Switzerland: Karger, 2001.

Thrangu, K. *Essentials of Mahamudra.* Somerville, MA: Wisdom Publications, 2004.

Thompson, E. *Between Ourselves.* UK: Imprint Academic, 2001.

Toga, A.W. and Mazziotta, J. C. *Brain Mapping.* San Diego, CA: Academic Press.

Winnicott, D.W. *The Maturational Processes and the Facilitating Environment.* Madison, CT: International Universities Press, 1965.